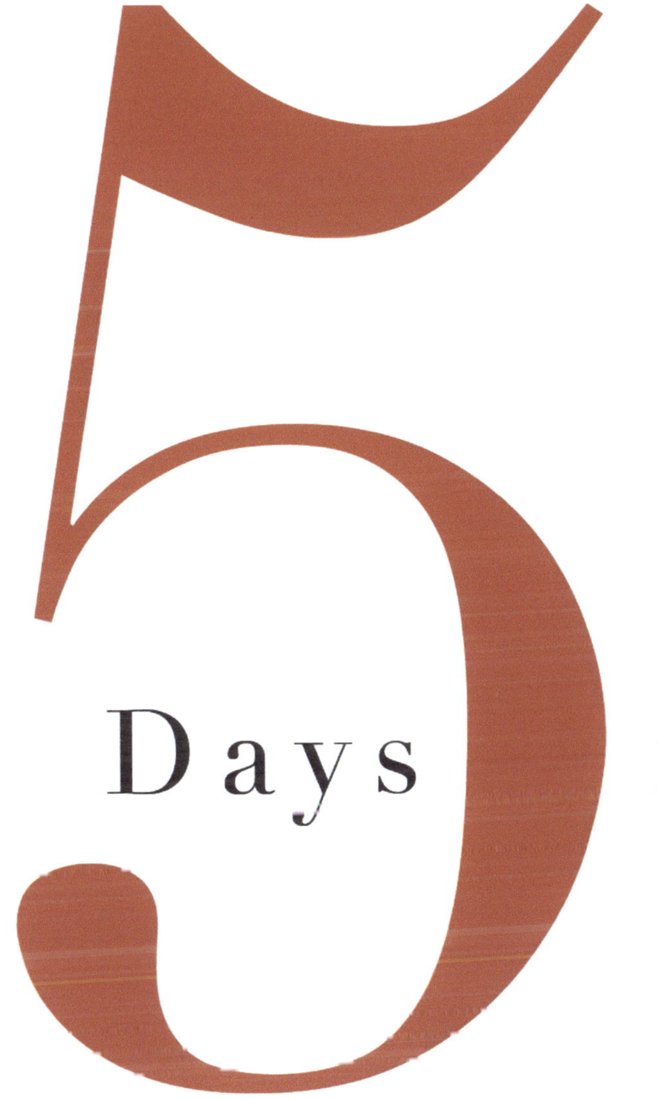

Days 5 in New York

a photographer's journey

5 Days in New York: A Photographer's Journey

Published by: Shiftig Gears Publications, Ashland, Oregon
Interior & Cover Design by: Jeff Altemus, Align Visual Arts & Communication
Edited by: Valerie Sullivan Loss

ISBN: 978-0-9899404-2-9

Printed in the United States of America

For Jay Maisel.
You have influenced many lives. You have changed mine.

a week with jay maisel

Jay Maisel has been shooting in the streets of New York City and around the world for more than sixty years. His work is about light, gesture, and often vibrant color. During the past half century, he has photographed many celebrities, from Marilyn Monroe to Miles Davis. His unforgettable images have been used for advertising, editorial, and album covers. Jay has the eye of an impressionist and launches photography into the arena of fine art. He sees the world, and the things most of us pass by, with phenomenal insight. At eighty-two, he remains a legend and a Renaissance man.

After watching documentaries that examined the way Maisel works and offered glimpses into the way he thinks, I knew I wanted to crawl inside the man's brain. On his website, I read glowing testimonials from former students. Some made almost evangelical claims that he had even made them better people. Then I read further: "Leave your ego at the door." I worried about what I would be in for. I knew I was ready for a much-needed artistic transformation, a transfusion. What I did not know was how enjoyable that journey would be.

At precisely 8:30 Monday morning, I stood on the steps of Jay's studio-residence: a retired 35,000 square foot Germanic bank building on the corner of Bowery and Spring streets. The six-story building was well tagged with bold graffiti. When I touched the weathered wooden door, I felt as though I was about to enter a historical church instead of an old bank. I pushed the last-century doorbell, half expecting to be greeted by a monk, the guardian of the sacred inner sanctum. Instead, Jamie, a happy-faced studio manager, welcomed me inside and led me onto an indoor basketball court that was now a part of the former bank's lobby. I stood in the middle of the coolest studio and gallery I had ever seen, surrounded by phenomenal photography. I knew instantly that I had just entered the domain of someone I wanted to know, someone I wanted to turn my photographic soul over to for a gentle cleansing. Little did I know that the cleansing, the scrubbing, would be deep and anything but gentle.

I introduced myself to a few of the other pilgrims, many from various parts of the USA, some from other countries. We were all here for much the same reason; we hoped for a merciful deliverance into a brand new universe.

WITH COFFEE IN HAND, all 10 of us sat around a long table, filling out questionnaires that asked things like, "How much equipment do you take on a shoot?" and "How do you know when you have taken a good shot?" By the end of the sheet, I realized they all boiled down to one question: "Why are you here—on this planet?"

Jay arrived, tall and trim, with his glasses perched on his forehead. As he greeted us, my first thought was, "This guy is NOT eighty-two years old." He had the same energy and passion that radiates from his photographs. The nap time I had hoped would be part of our daily schedule would not be an option.

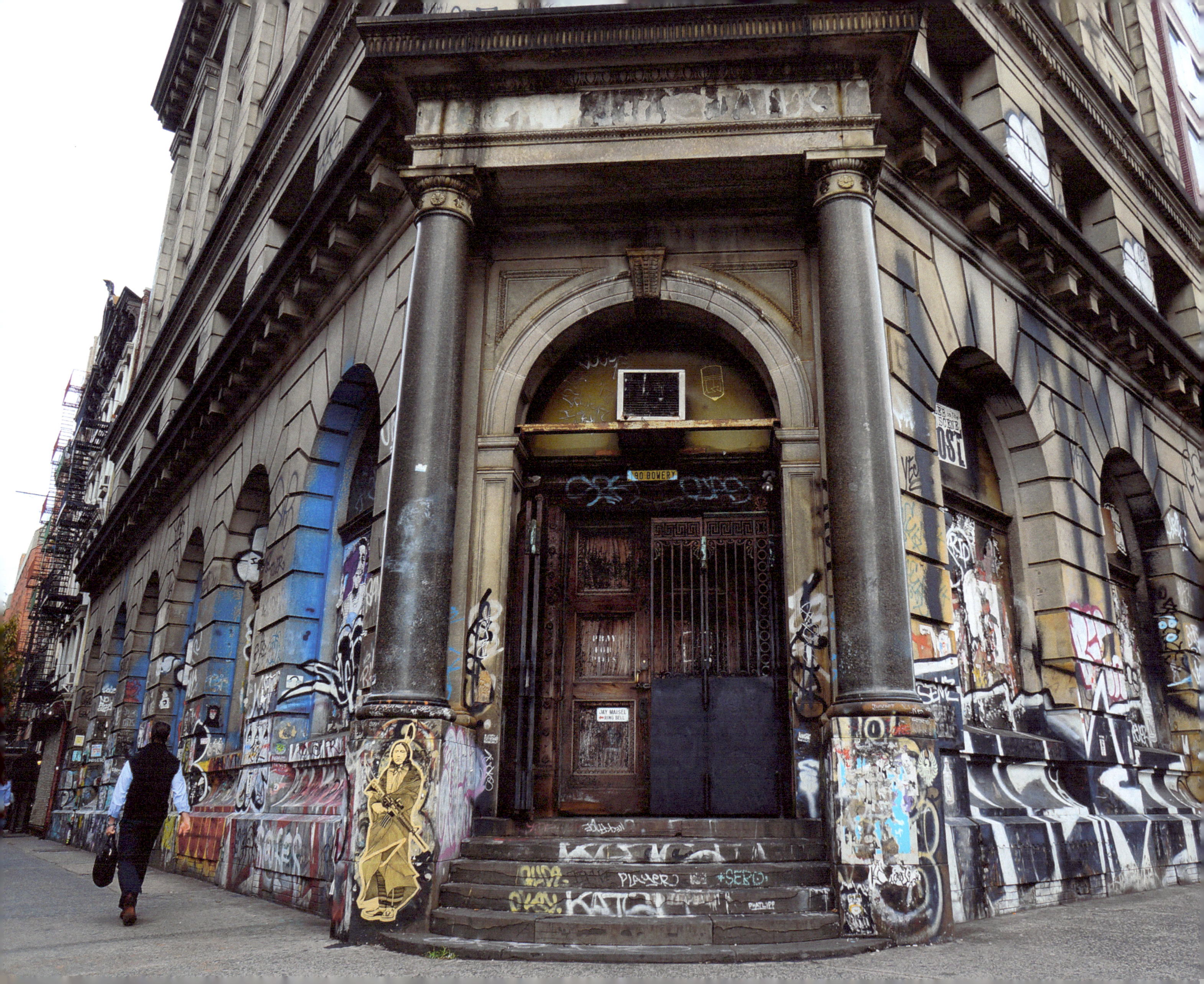

90 BOWERY
PRAY FOR PIPS
JAY MAISEL
RING BELL

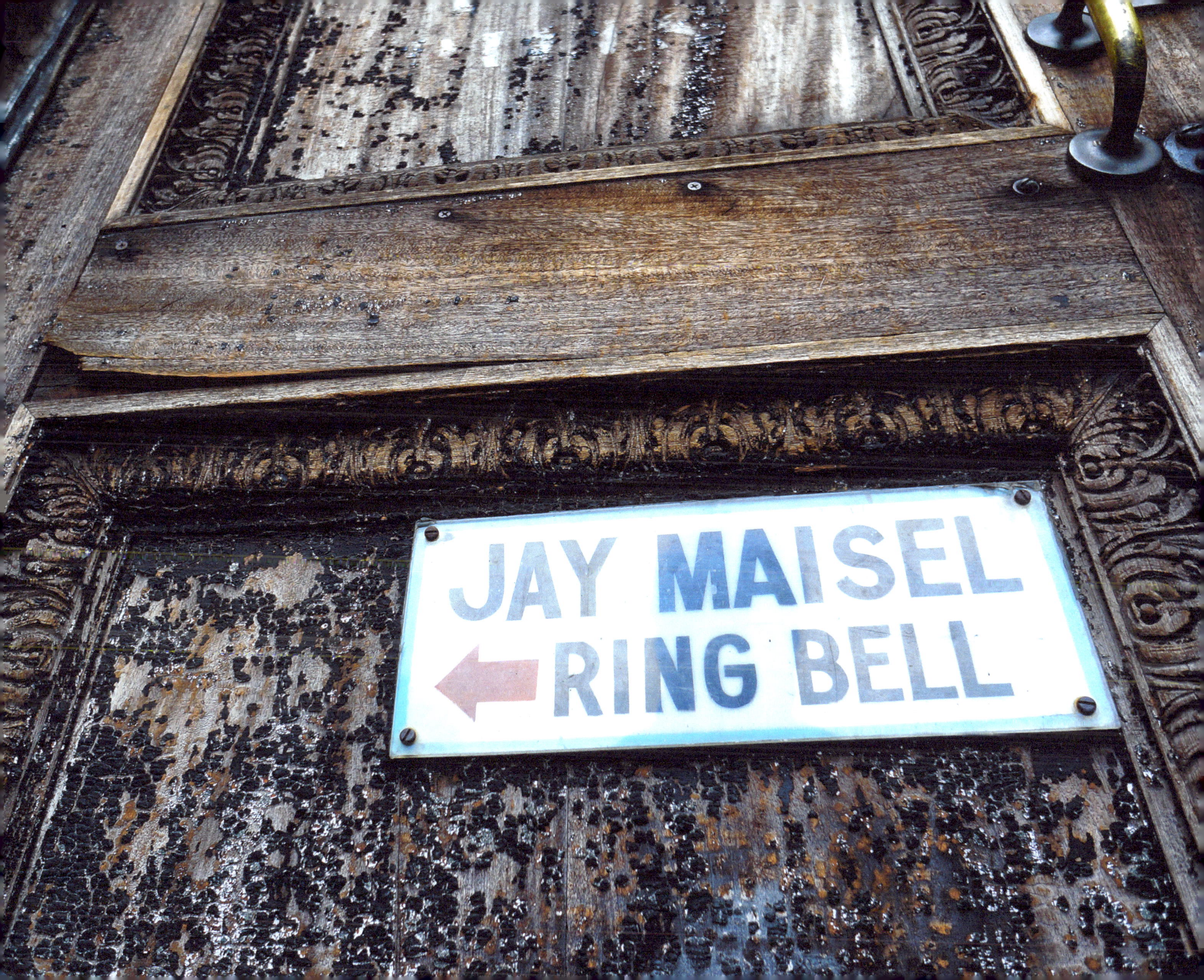

JAY MAISEL
RING BELL

Then it came time to go around the table and introduce ourselves. I was charged up and excited to tell everyone about my 3o years as a professional photographer and all about my books on Cambodia and New Orleans. I soon realized that I had started off on the wrong foot, setting myself up as an oversized target of critique. Jay looked into my eyes and asked, simply, "Then, why are you here?"

I stammered in response, hoping for some reprieve. "I want to take my vision, my voice, to a higher level."

I should have taken his website advice to leave my ego at the door, in a far off land.

DURING THE NEXT 5 DAYS, we shot from dawn until 1o at night, up and down every street and alley we could find, sometimes in the rain, sometimes in the dark. That was the easy part. The more difficult part was when we would come inside and encircle the long table in the bank's conference room. Jay had us hand in a thumb drive with the "best" images we had shot during the previous day. Only 5 photographs from each student were allowed. Each student, then Jay, gave a raw critique as the photographs came up on a huge Samsung monitor that dominated the room. If you couldn't think of why the image sucked, he handed out a list of 32 reasons to choose from, volatile ammunition for anyone to use.

#3. It's boring. #14. It's a cliché. #2o. The image takes you on a trip that isn't worth it.

"Let the flogging begin," I often joked. Jay clicked through the work, always asking probing questions, with eyes that hungered for more.

The students' work was shown in alphabetical order. For the first time in my life, I wished my last name started with a "Z" instead of a "B." My images were always the first on the screen. Some heartless, blind idiot at the back end of the table, just out of my sight, hurled so many grenades that I could actually feel my body slipping under the table to safety. But the worst was when no one said a word, implying that your photograph wasn't even worthy of an opinion or a comment. That silence was deafening.

I DIDN'T RUN. I didn't get on the plane and go home. Instead, I shot. I listened. I inhaled every word that came out of Jay's mind. He became the professor I not only admired, but really liked, as he dished out a perfect blend of in-your-face-honesty and genuine warmth. I was humbled even more by the wonderful photographic talent that many of the others brought to the sessions. I learned almost as much from them as I did from Jay. As the days flew by, I wanted to slow time so I could taste every moment. I even grew to appreciate that blind idiot, just out of sight, at the back end of the table.

Christopher Briscoe, 2013

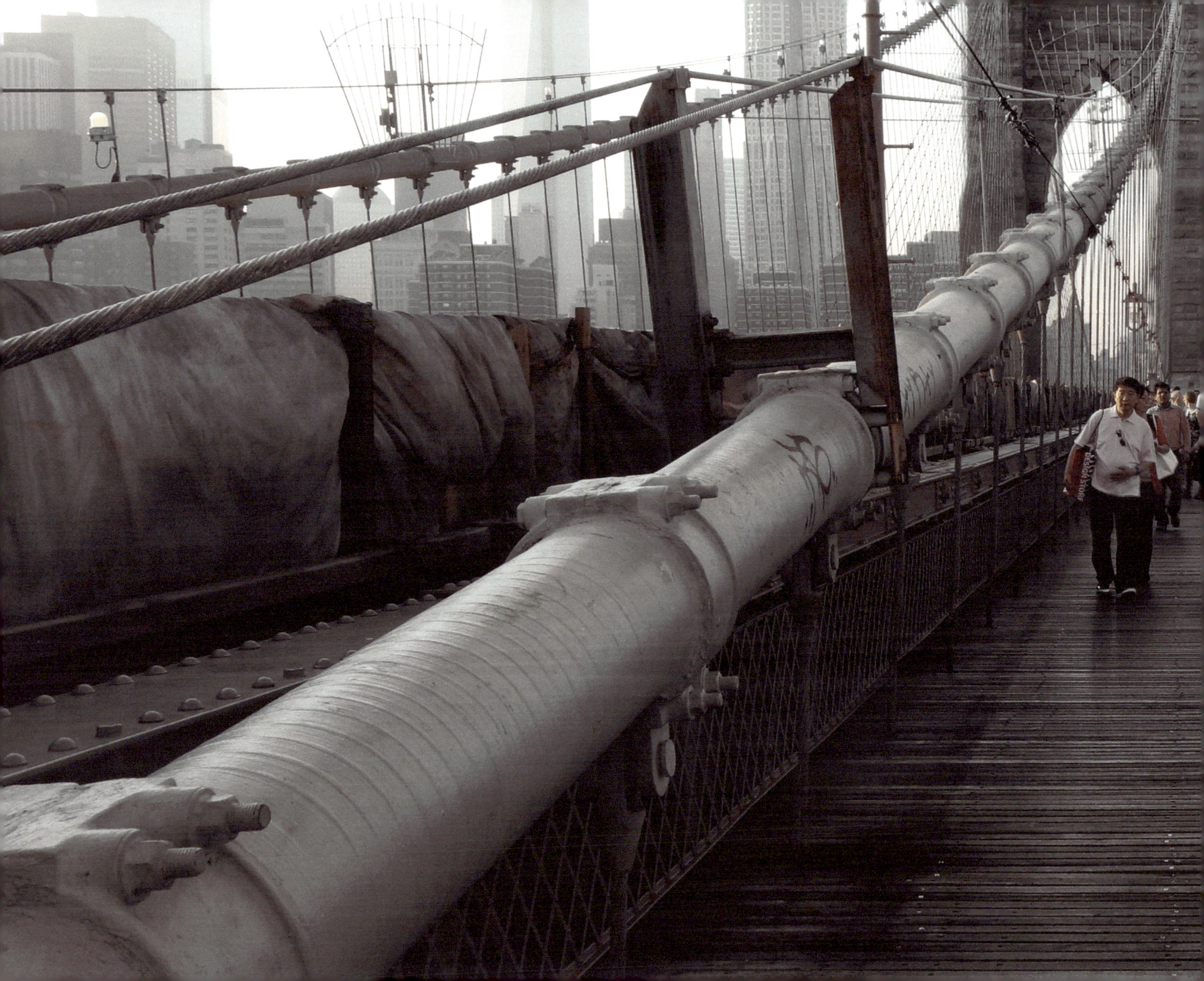

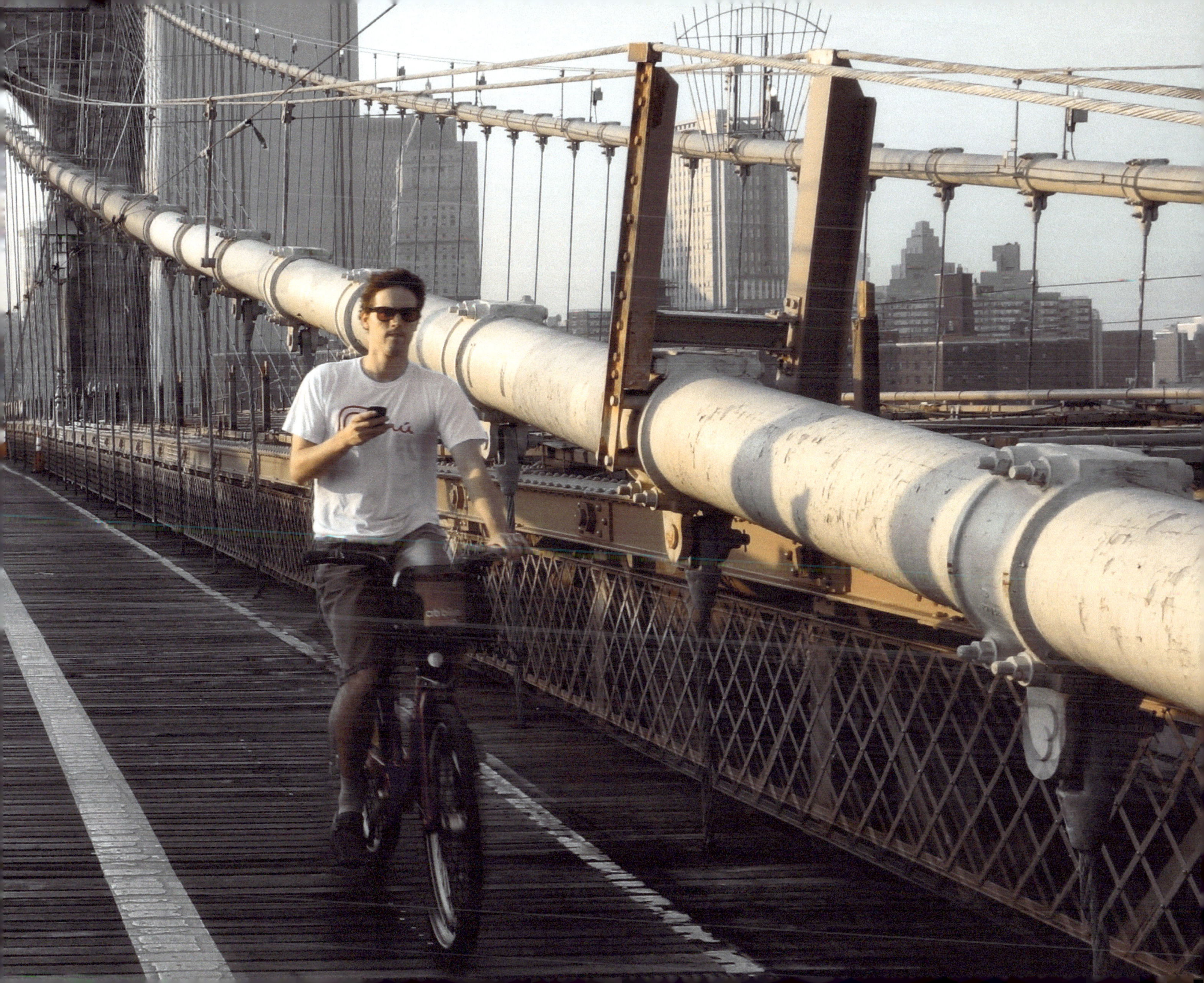

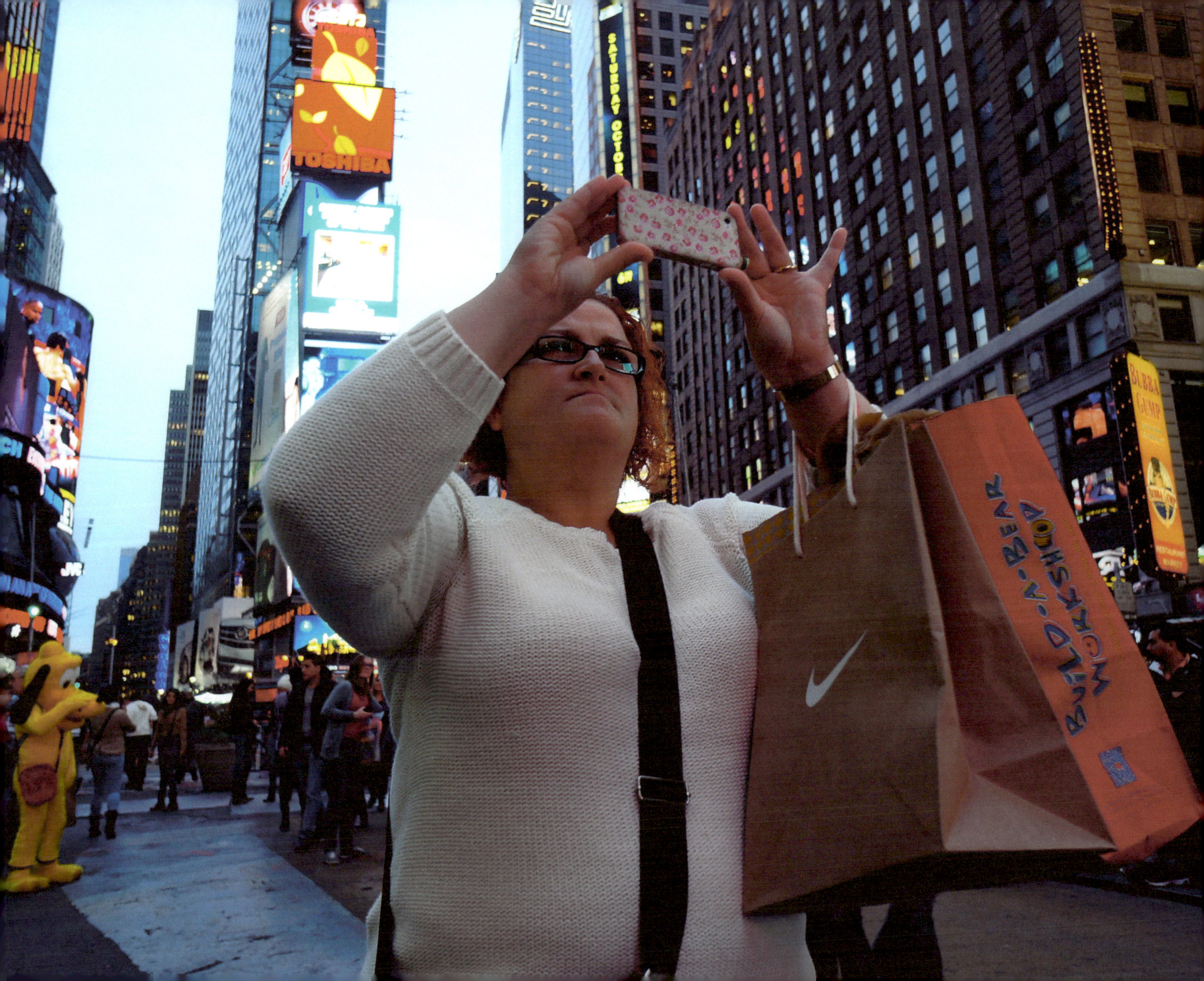
TOSHIBA
SATURDAY OCTOB
BUBBA
GUMP
BUILD-A-BEAR WORKSHOP

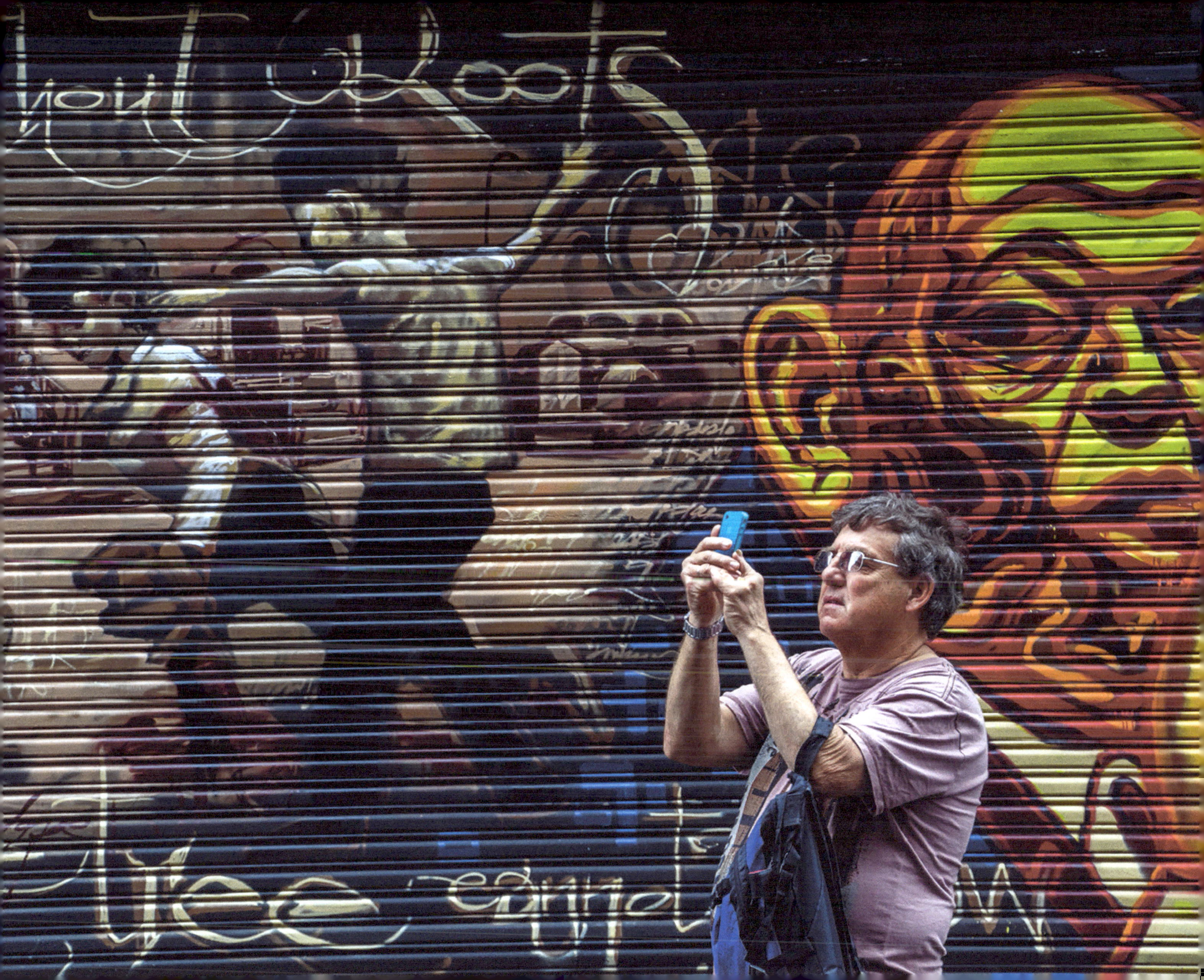

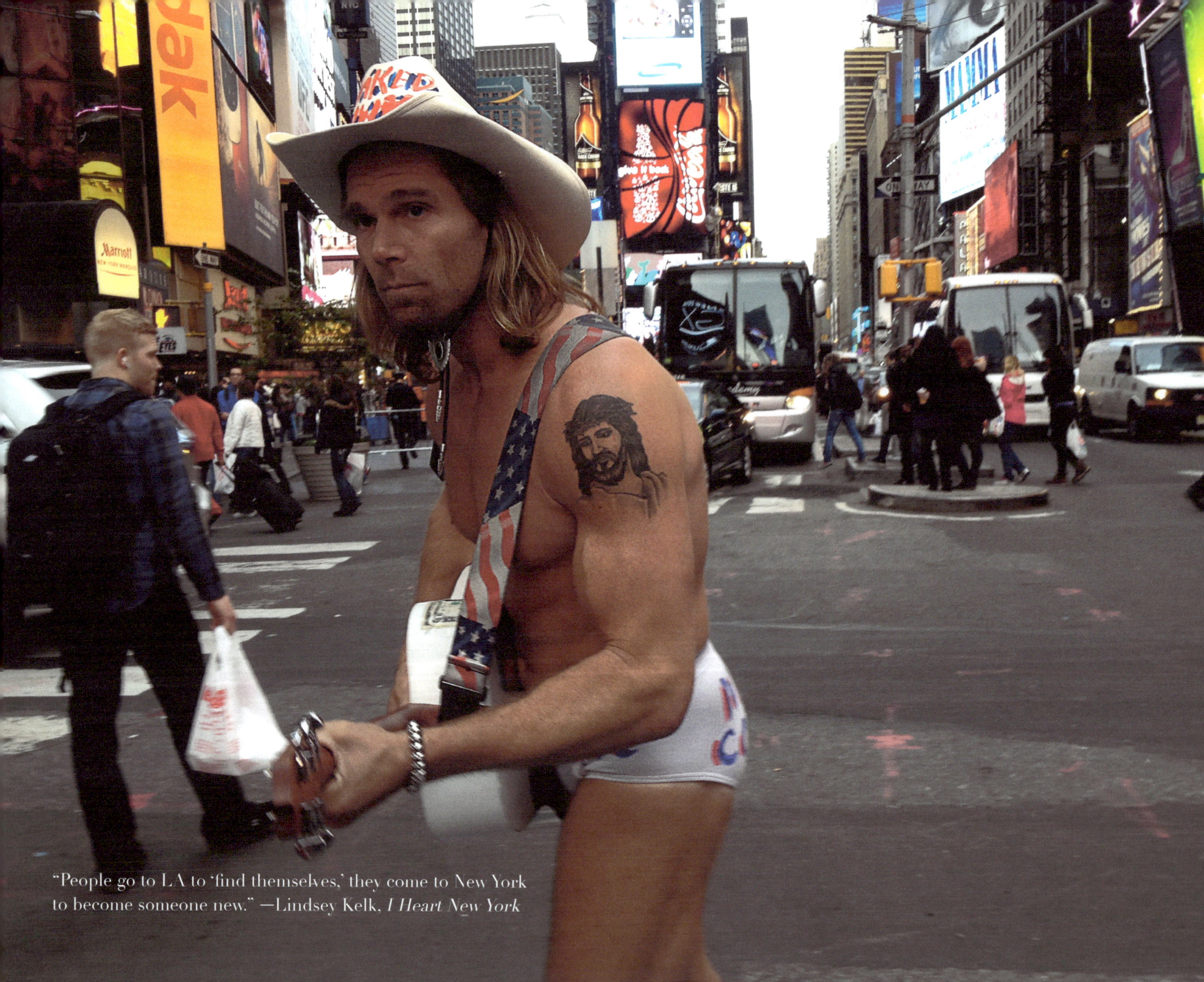

"People go to LA to 'find themselves,' they come to New York to become someone new." —Lindsey Kelk, *I Heart New York*

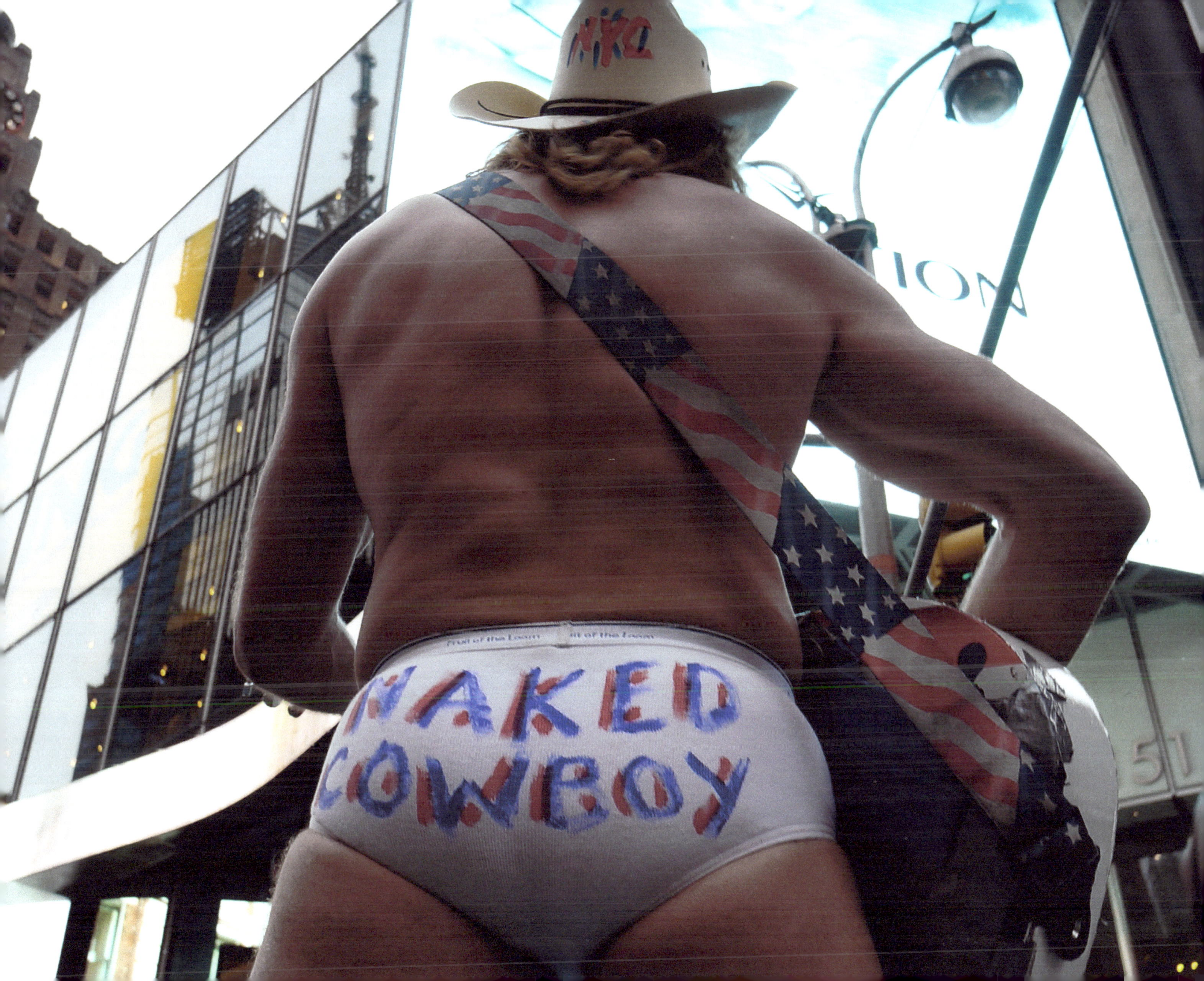

NYC
NAKED
COWBOY
Fruit of the Loom
ION
51

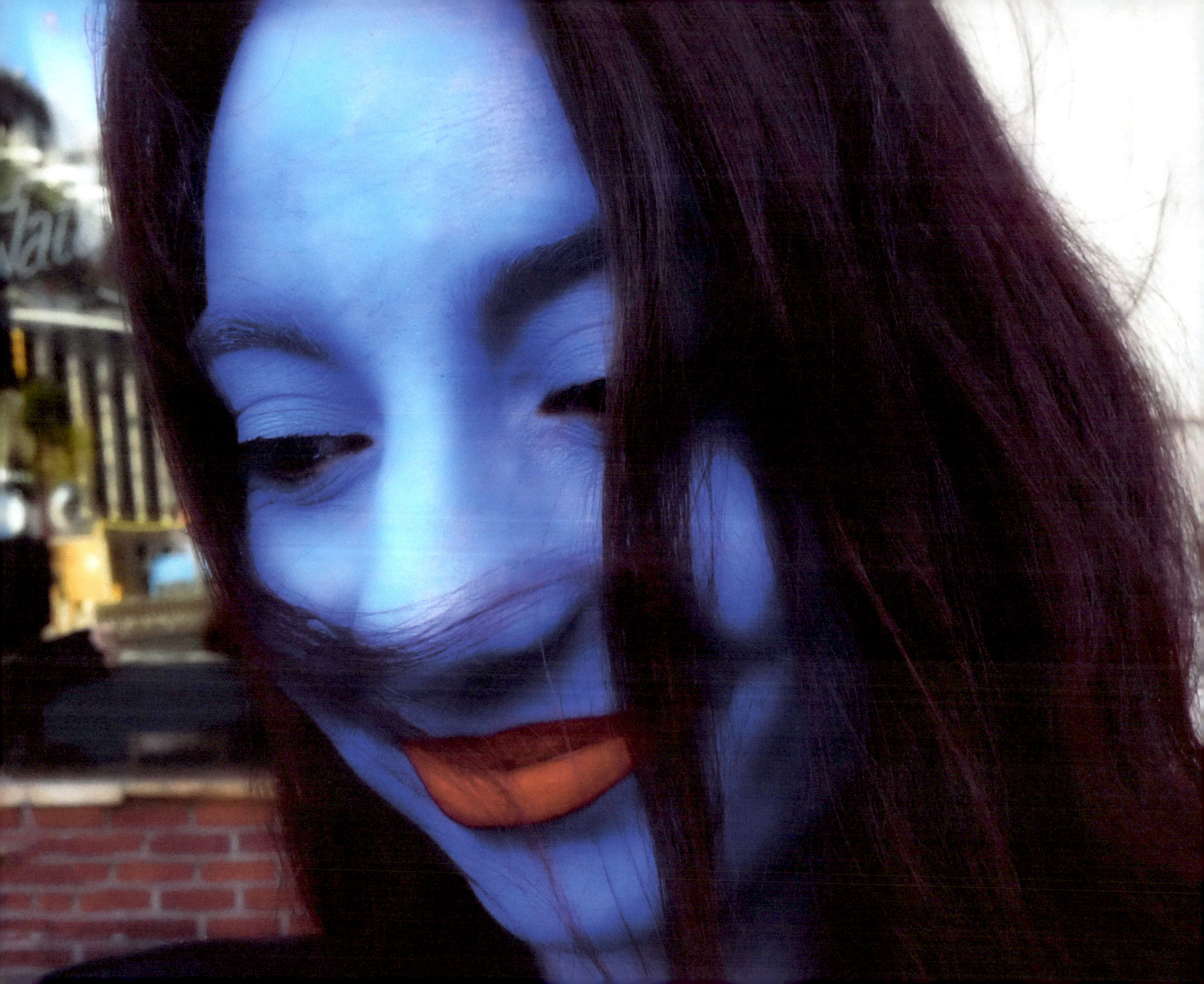

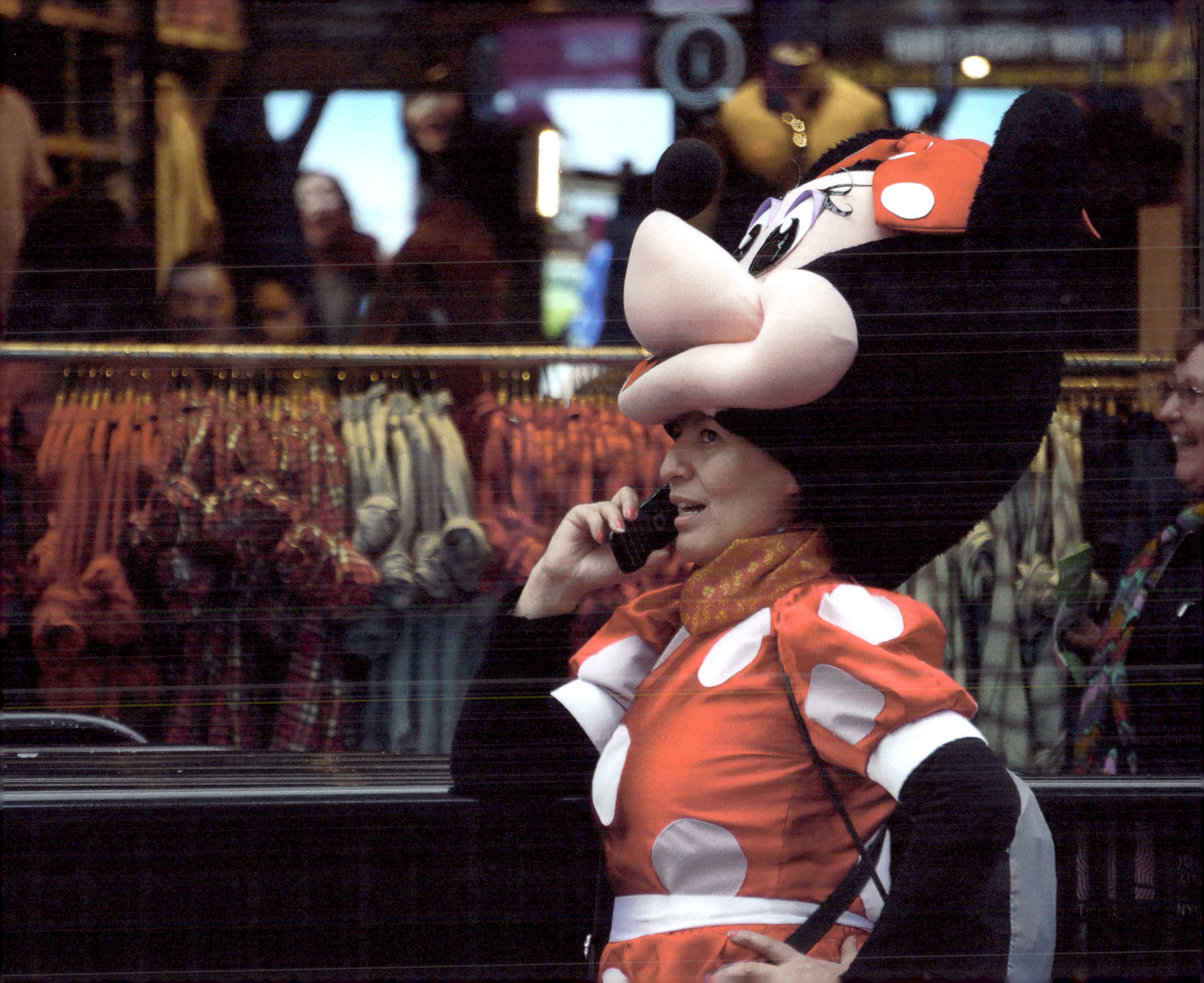

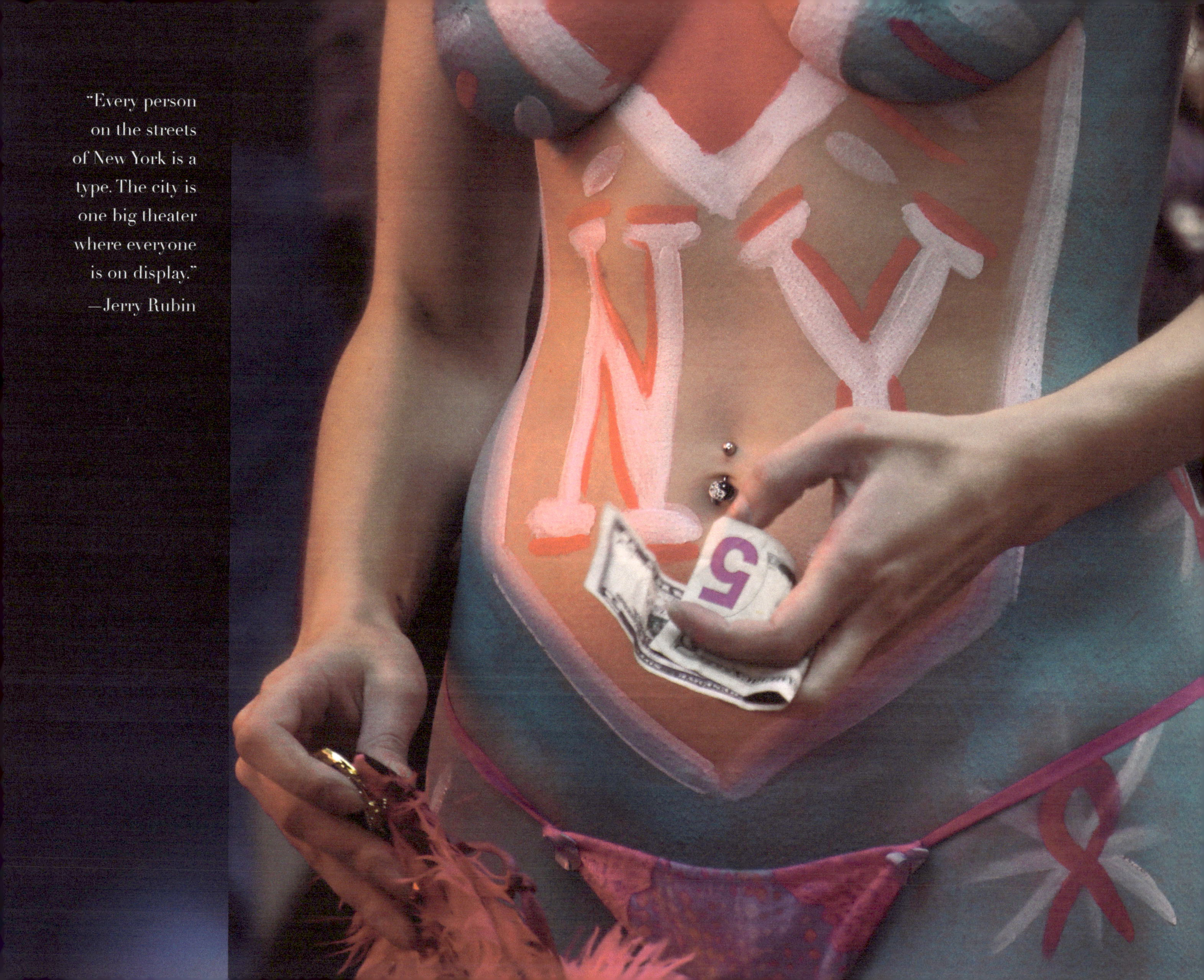

"Every person
on the streets
of New York is a
type. The city is
one big theater
where everyone
is on display."
—Jerry Rubin

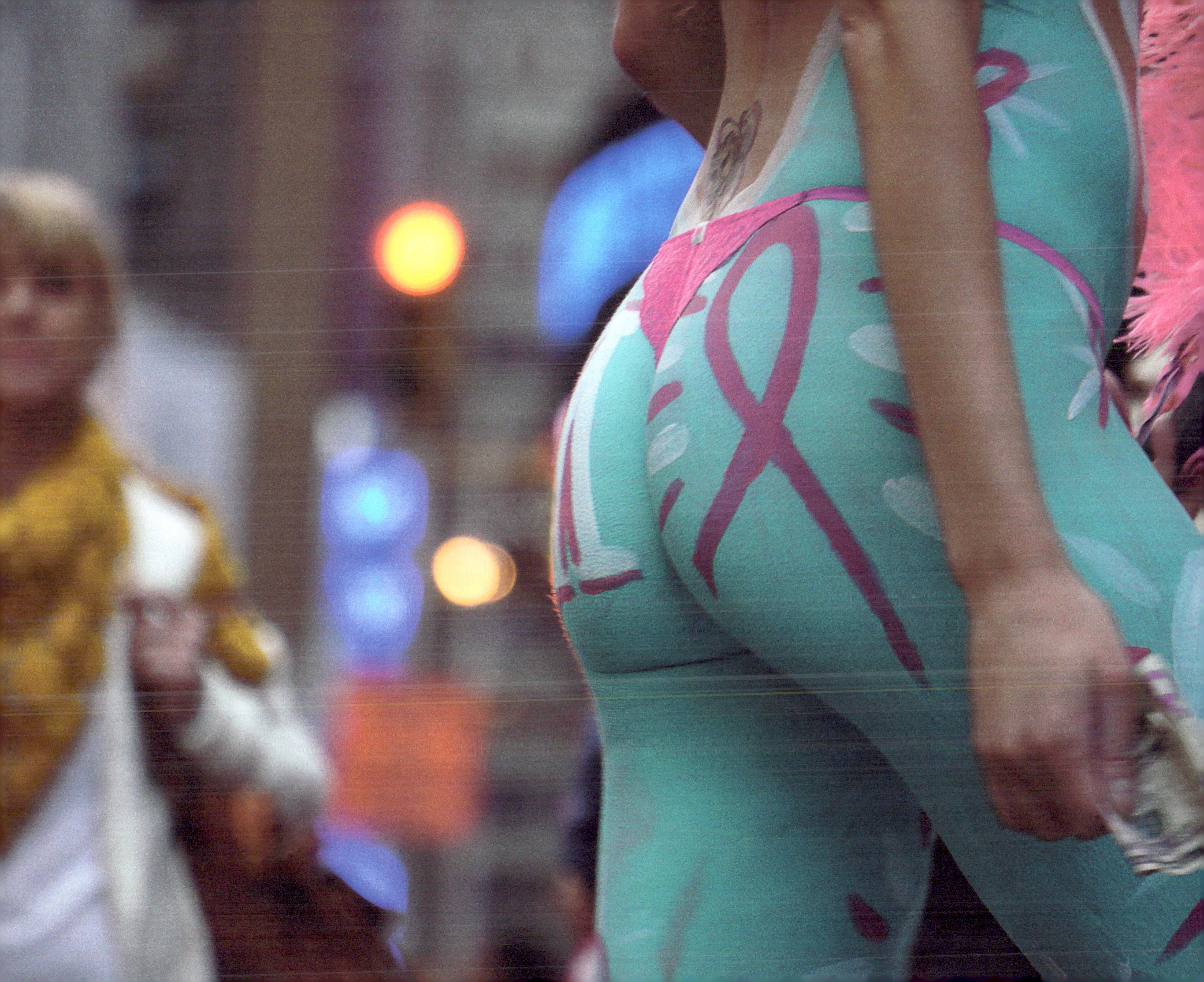

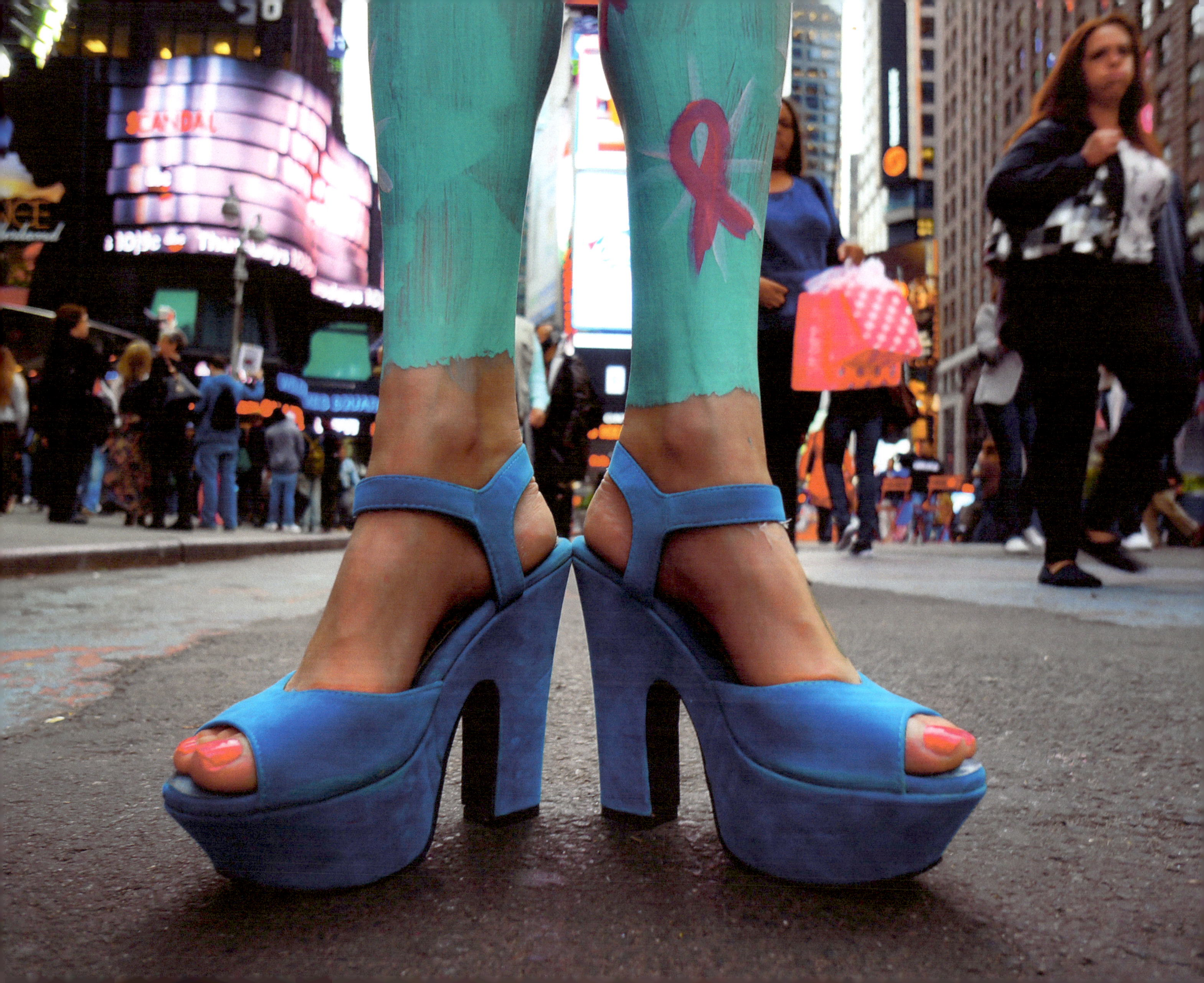

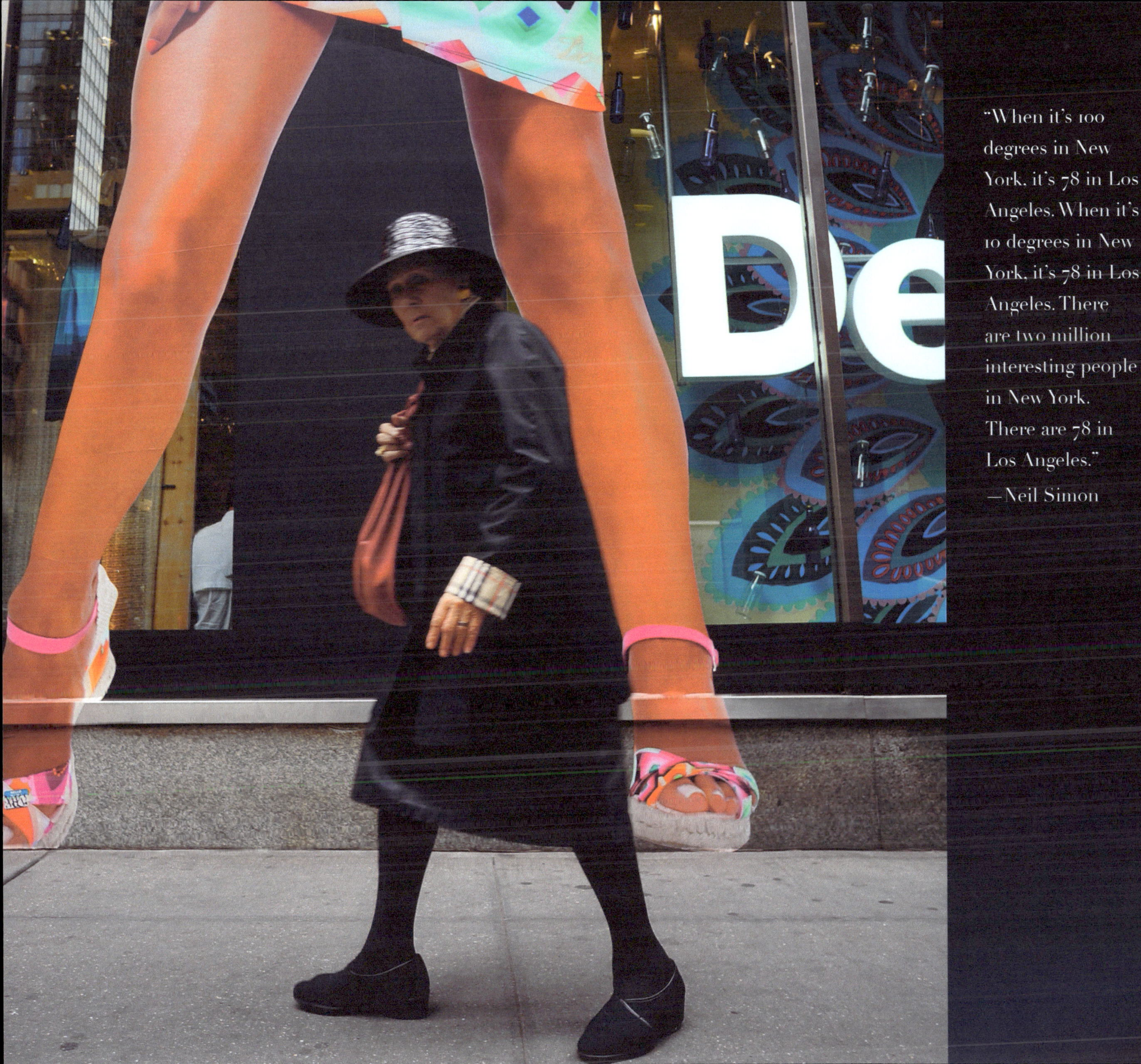
"When it's 100
degrees in New
York, it's 78 in Los
Angeles. When it's
10 degrees in New
York, it's 78 in Los
Angeles. There
are two million
interesting people
in New York.
There are 78 in
Los Angeles."
—Neil Simon

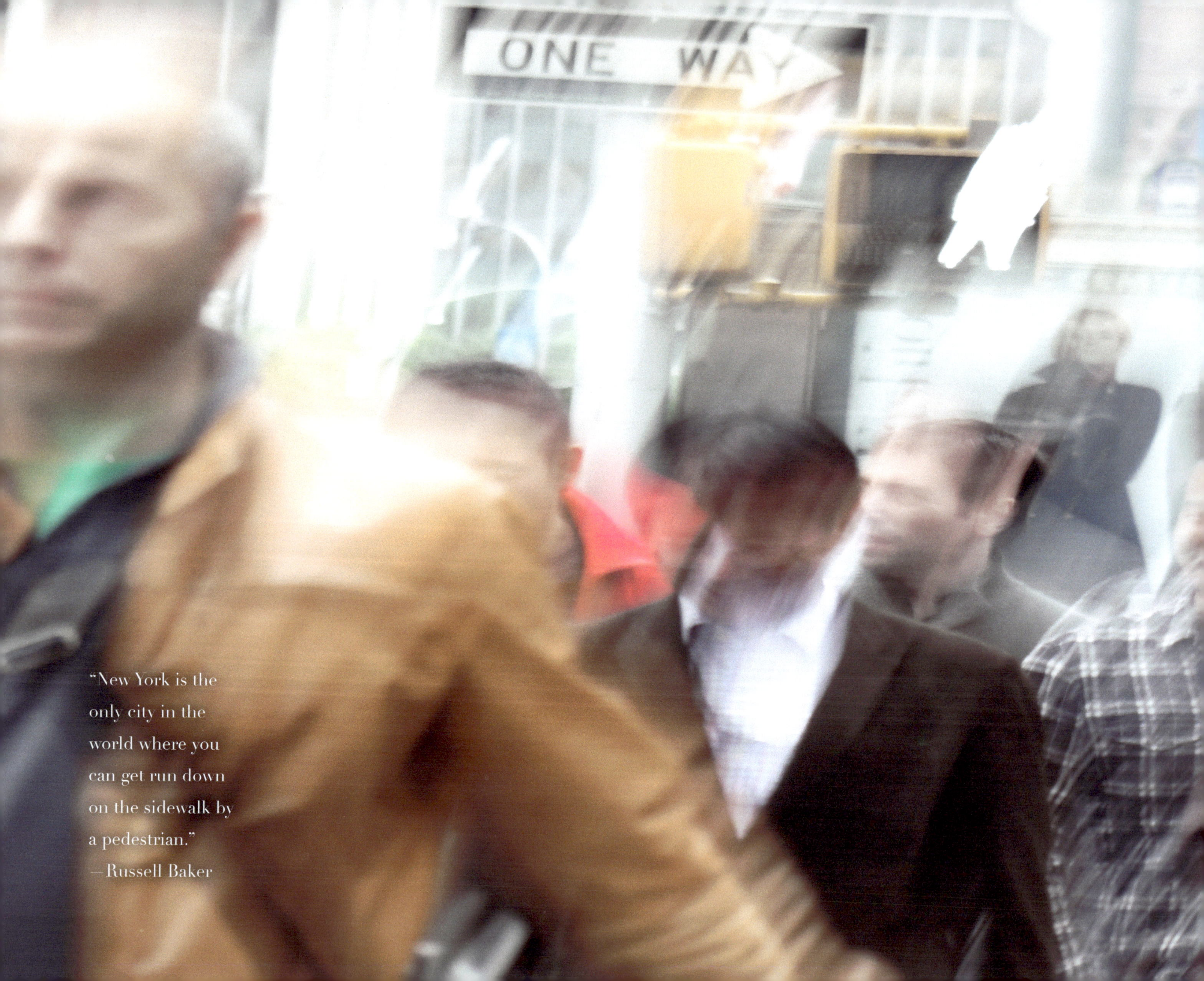
ONE WAY
"New York is the only city in the world where you can get run down on the sidewalk by a pedestrian."
—Russell Baker

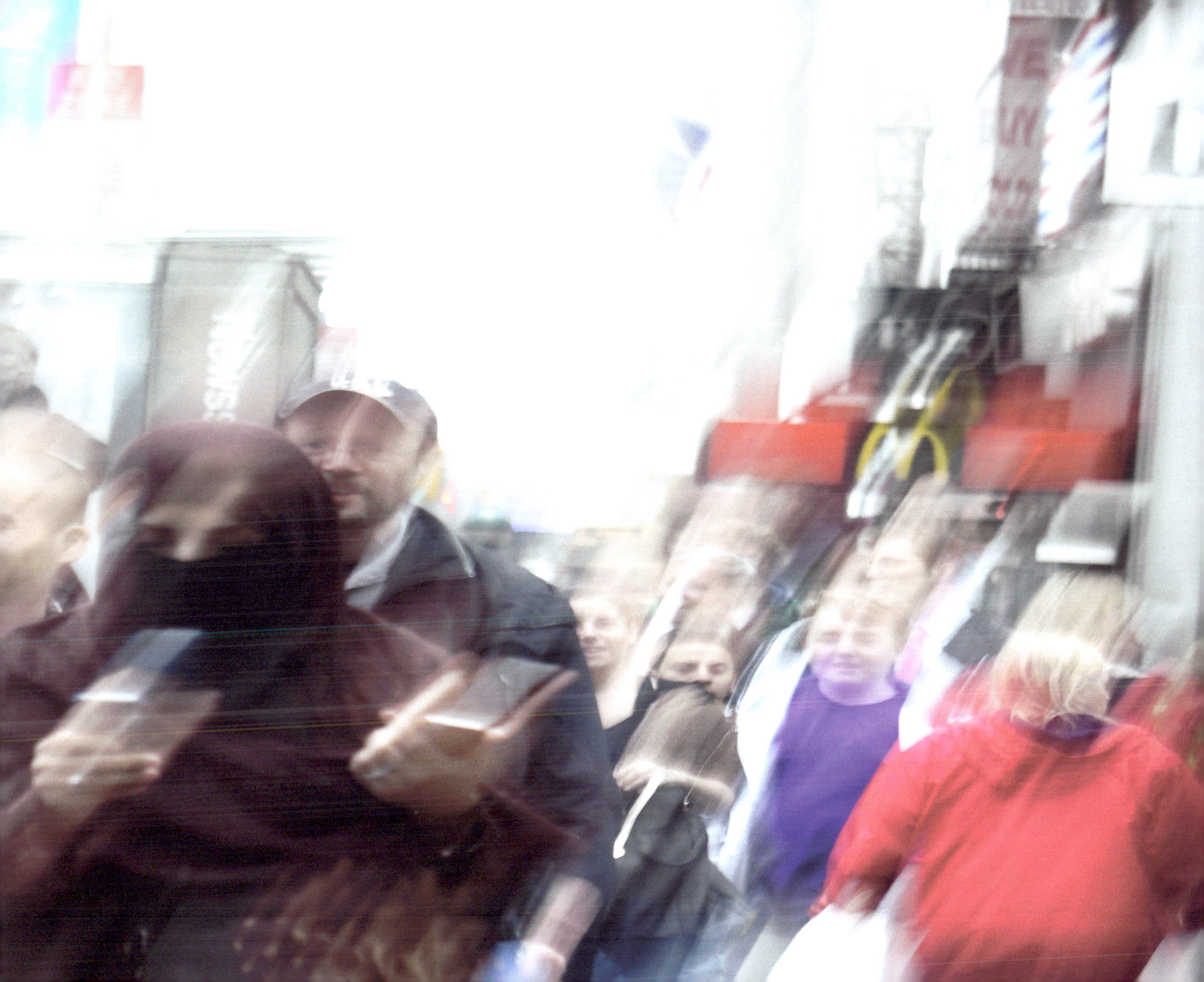

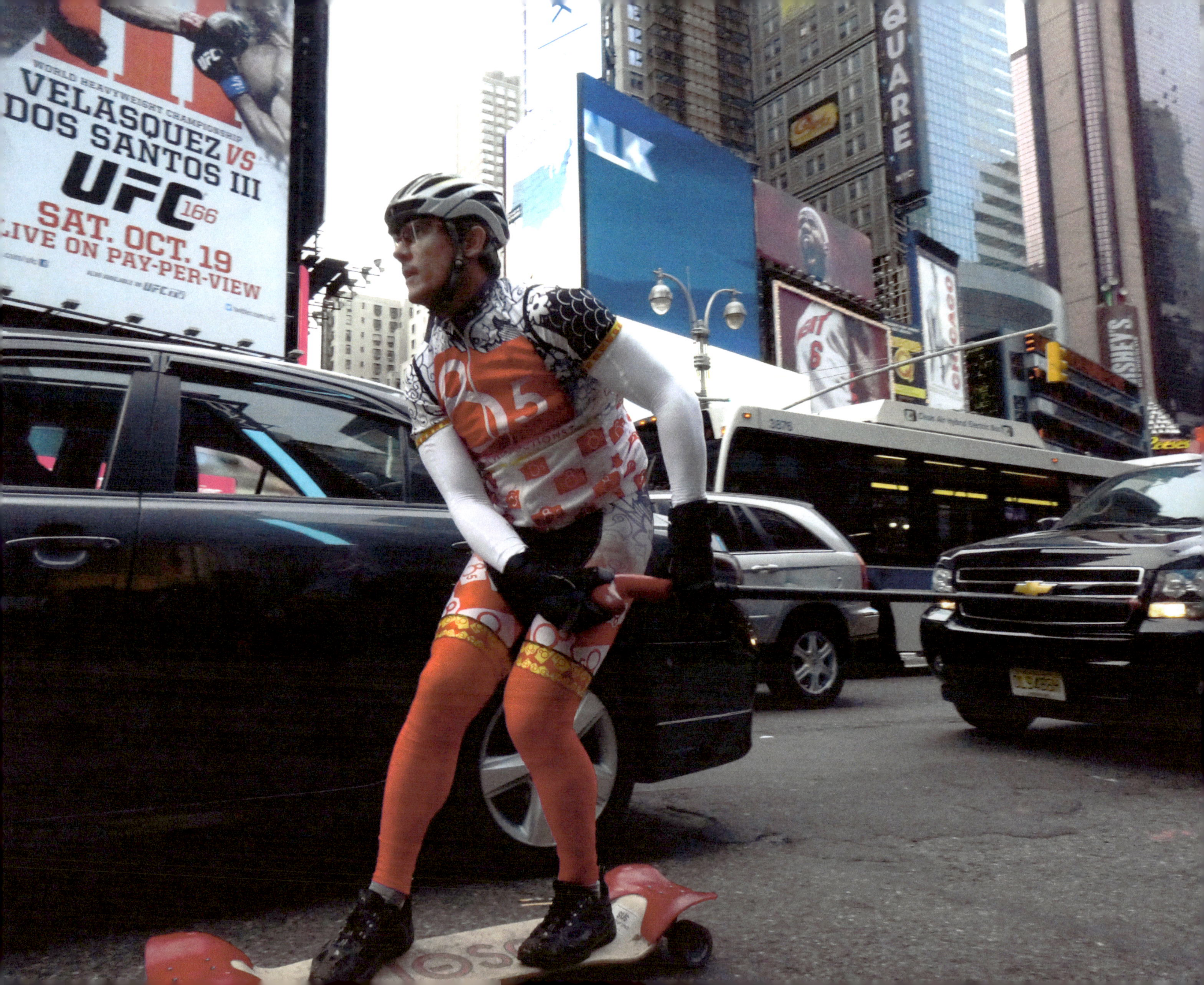

WORLD HEAVYWEIGHT CHAMPIONSHIP
VELASQUEZ VS
DOS SANTOS III
UFC 166
SAT. OCT. 19
LIVE ON PAY-PER-VIEW
QUARE
HERSHEY'S
HEAT
6

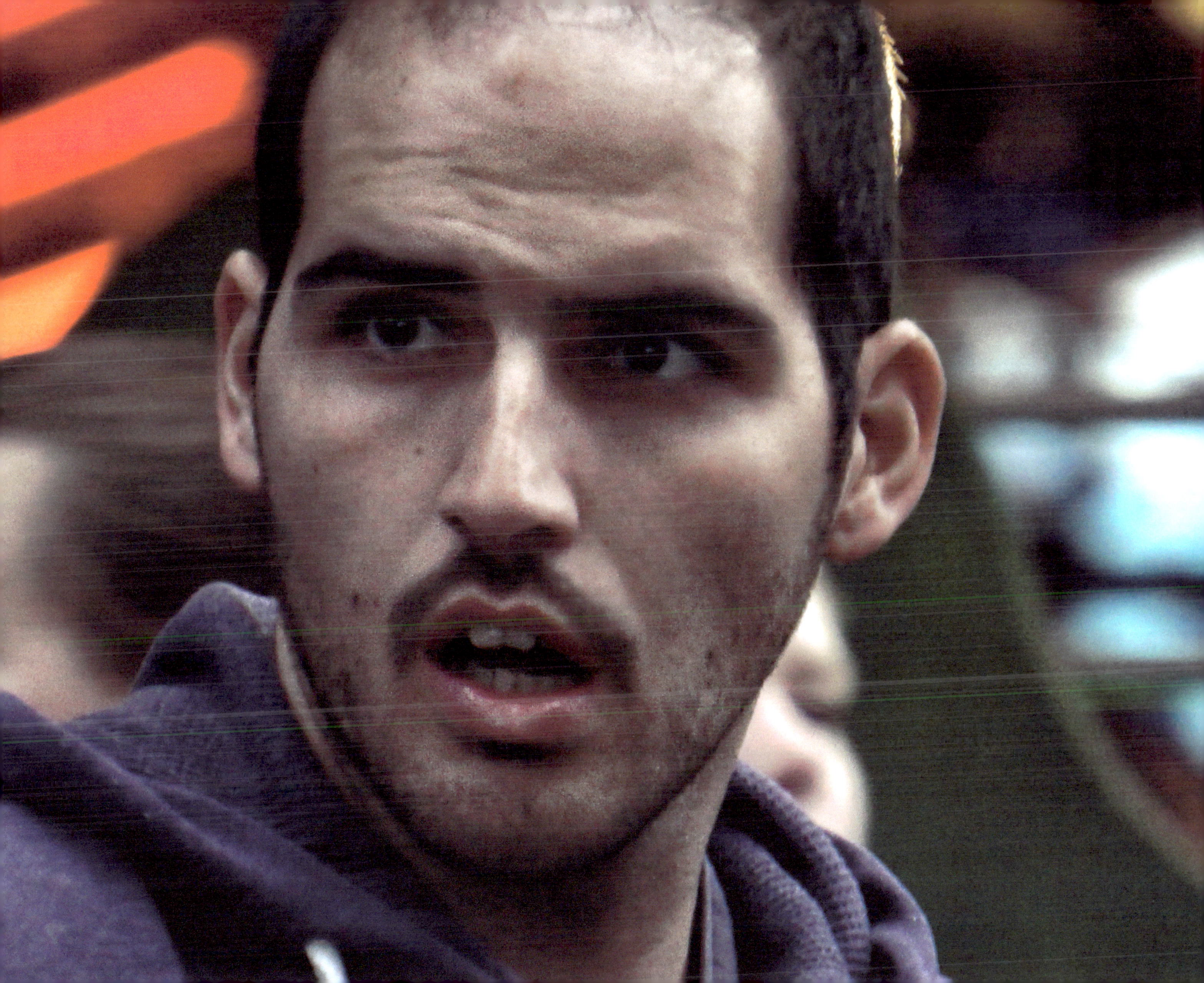

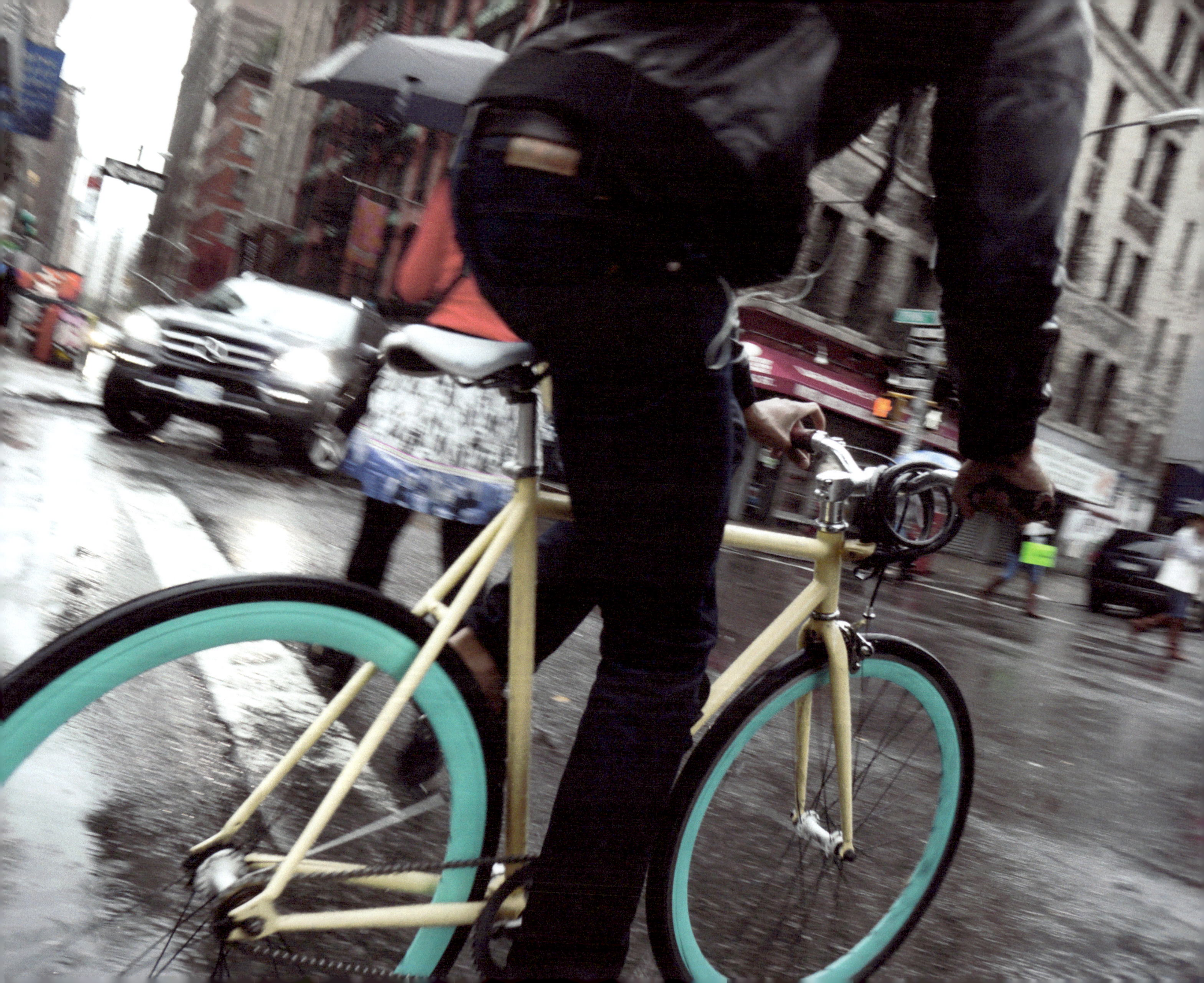

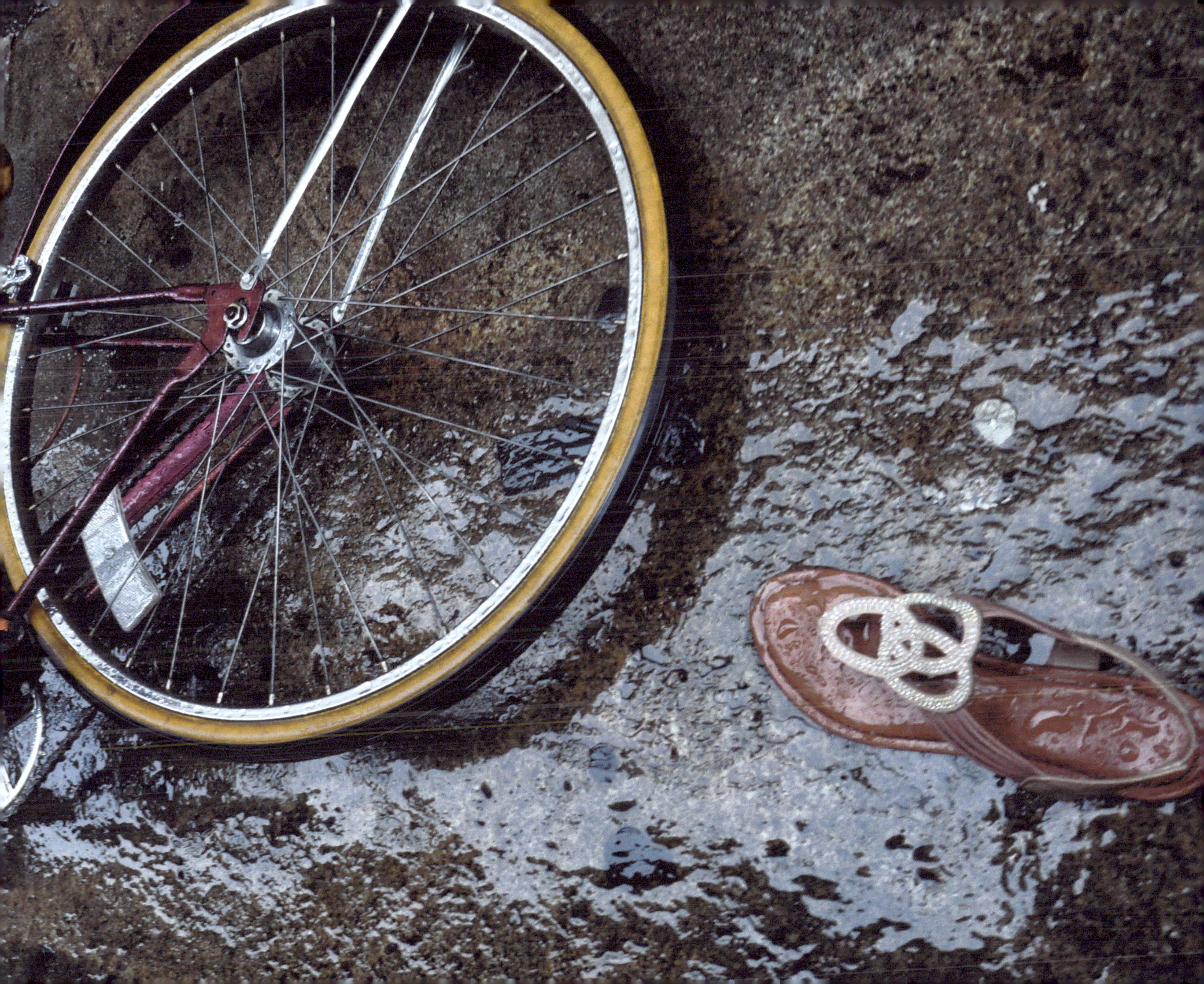

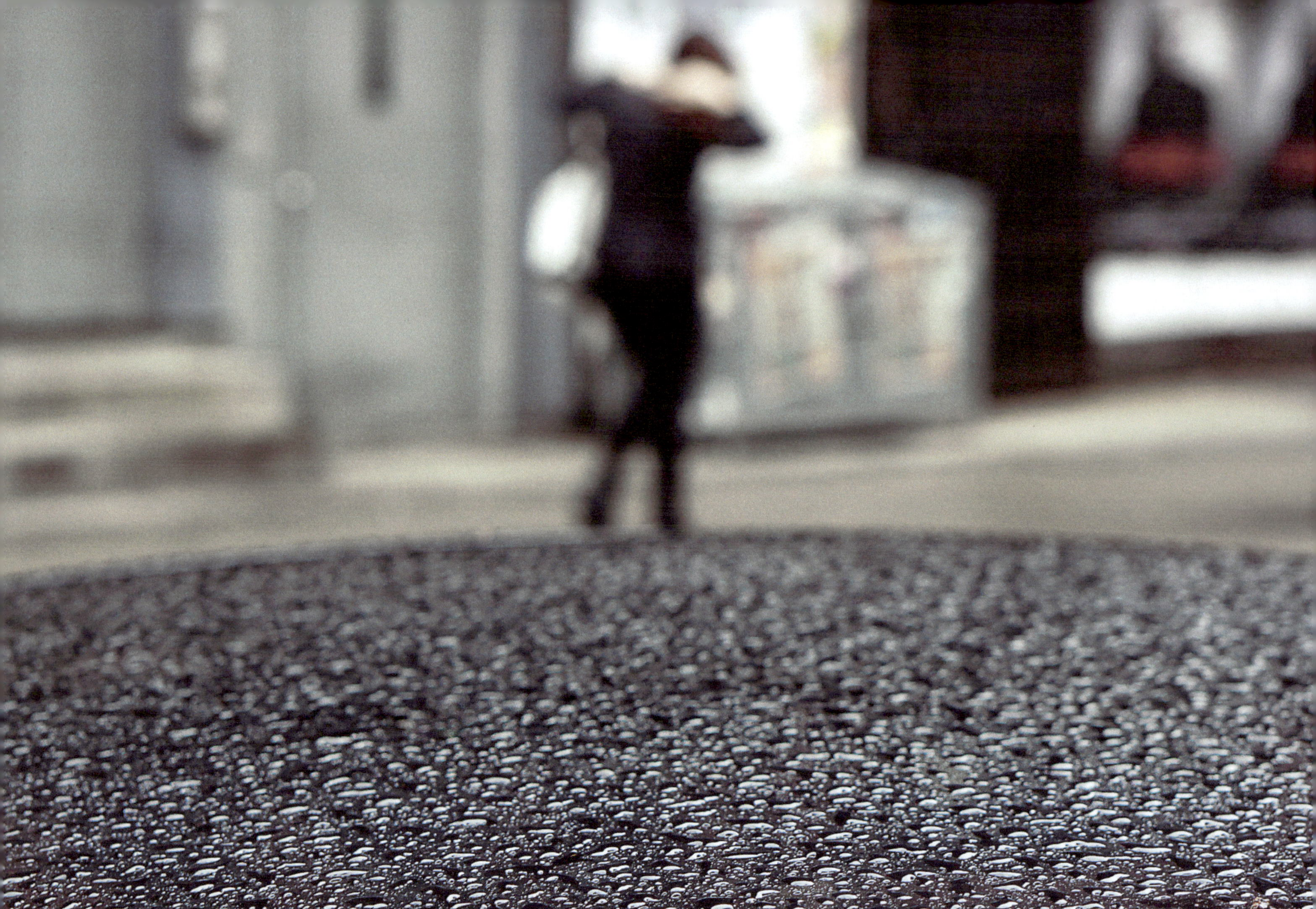

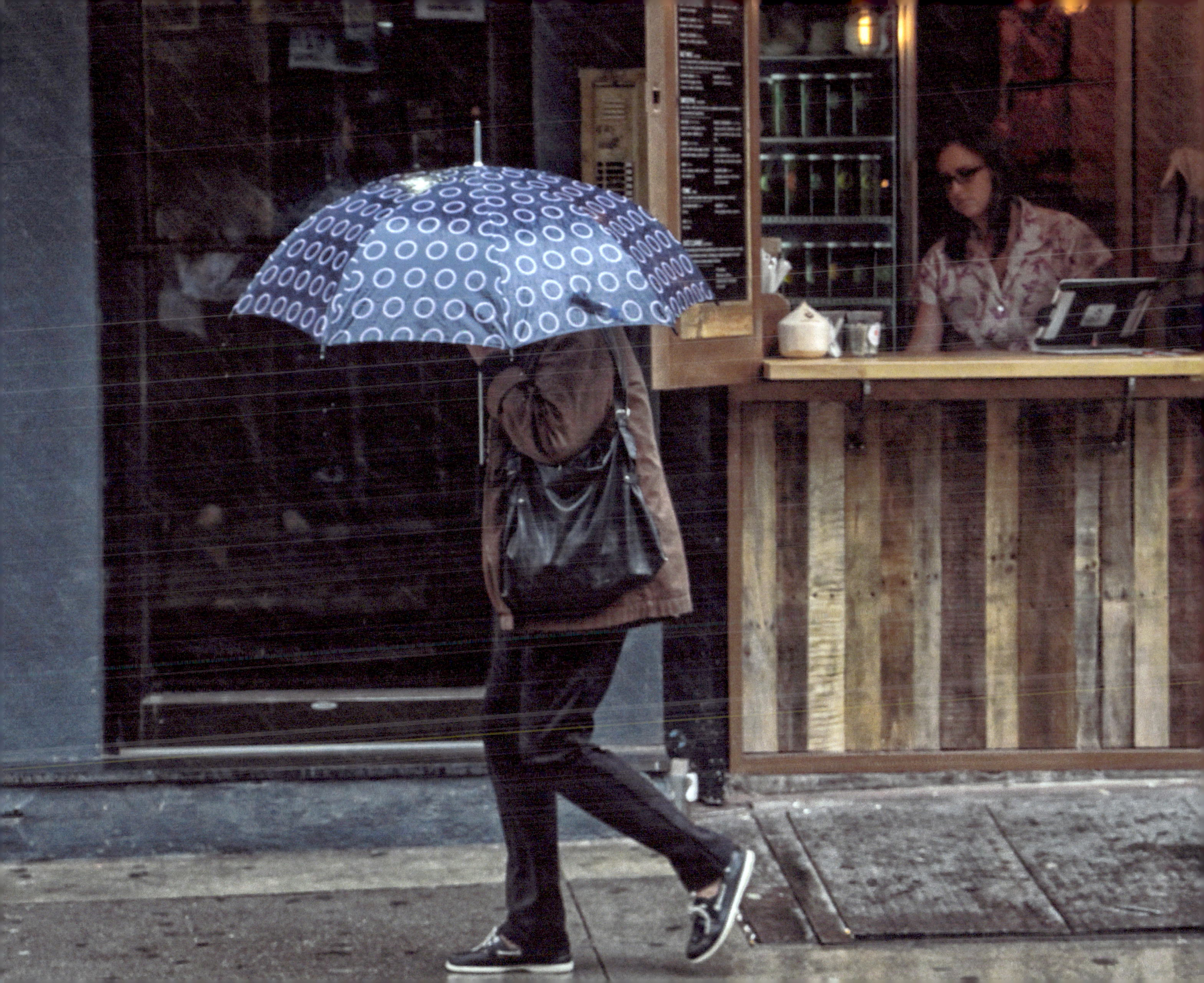

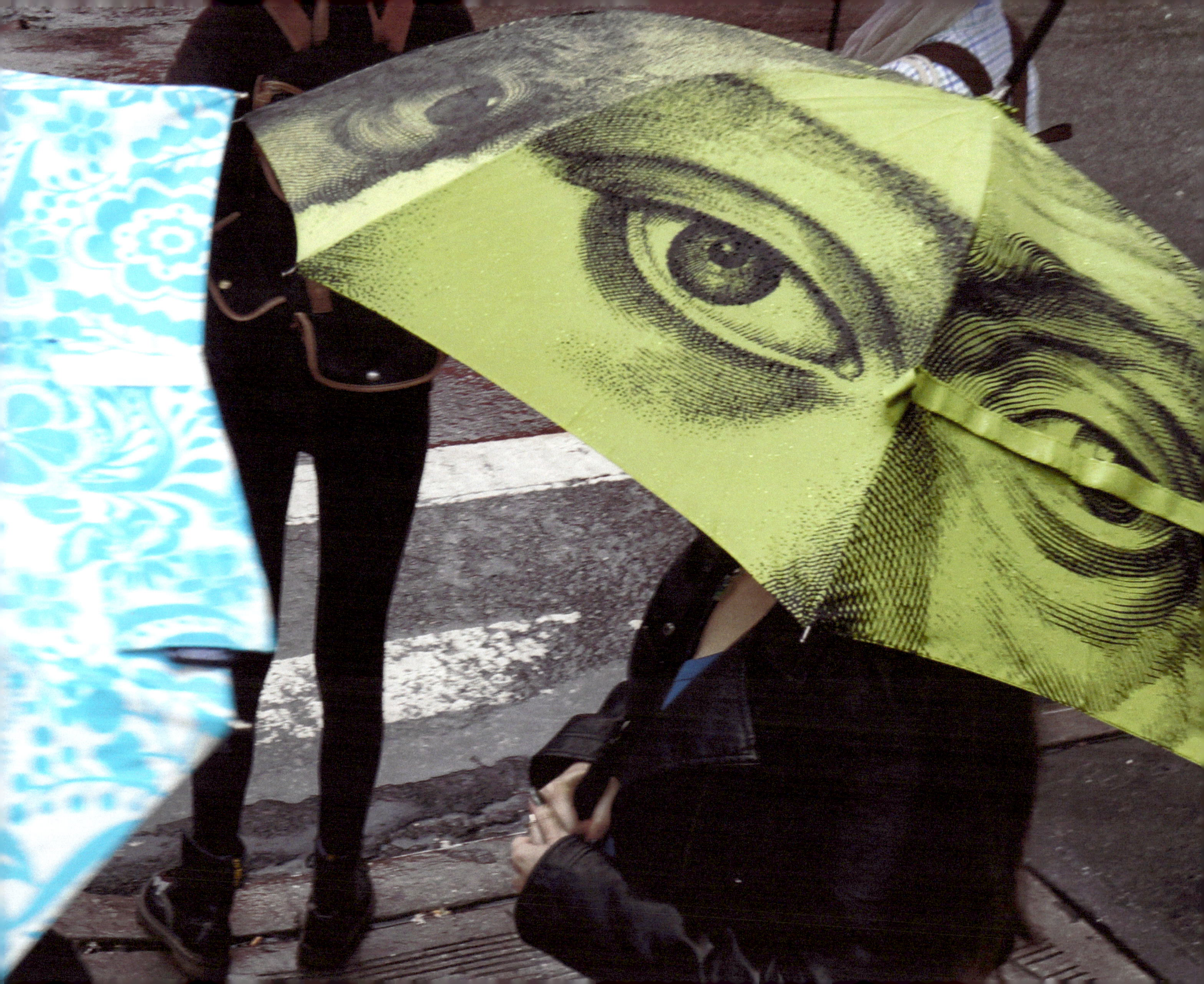

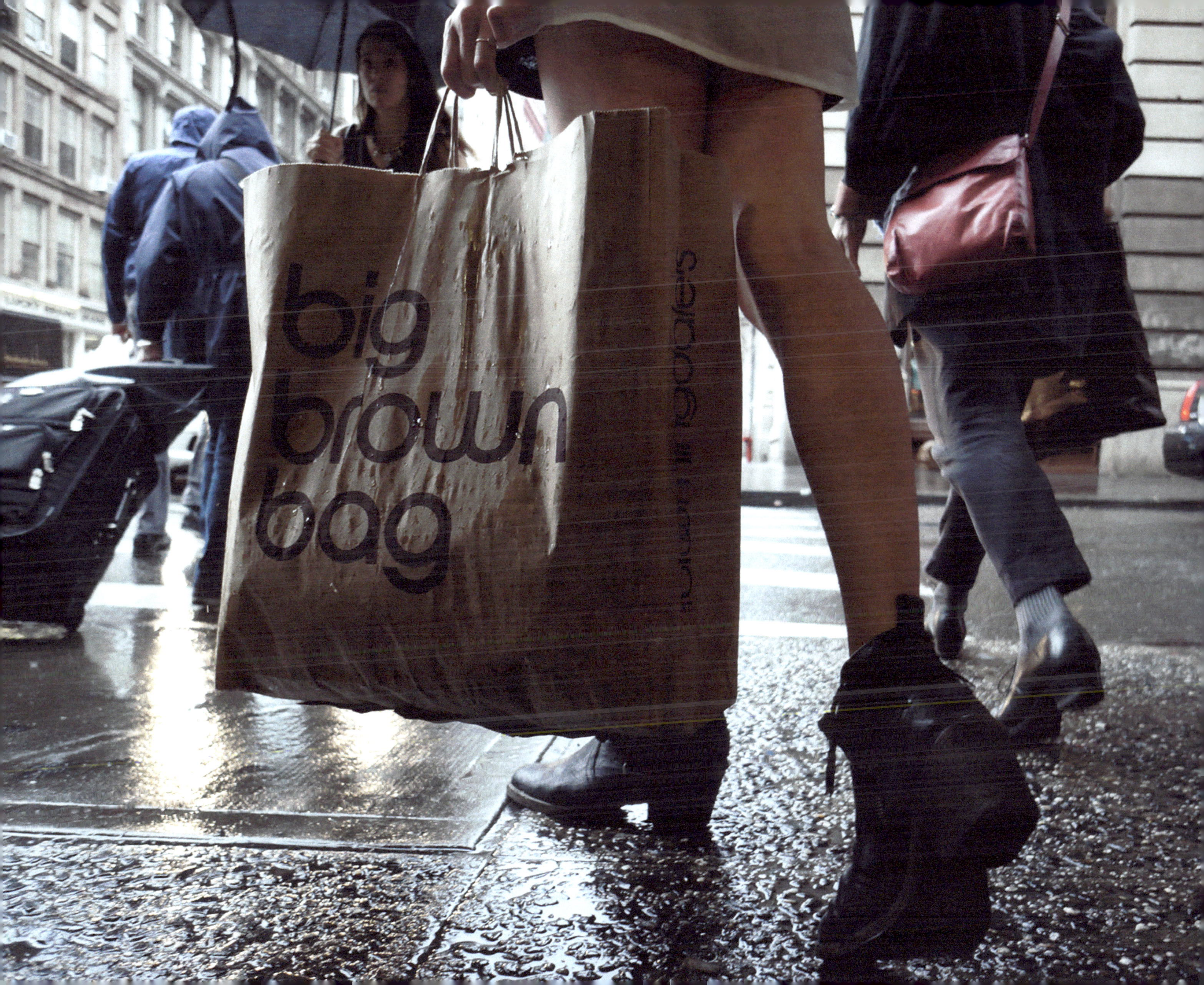
big
brown
bag

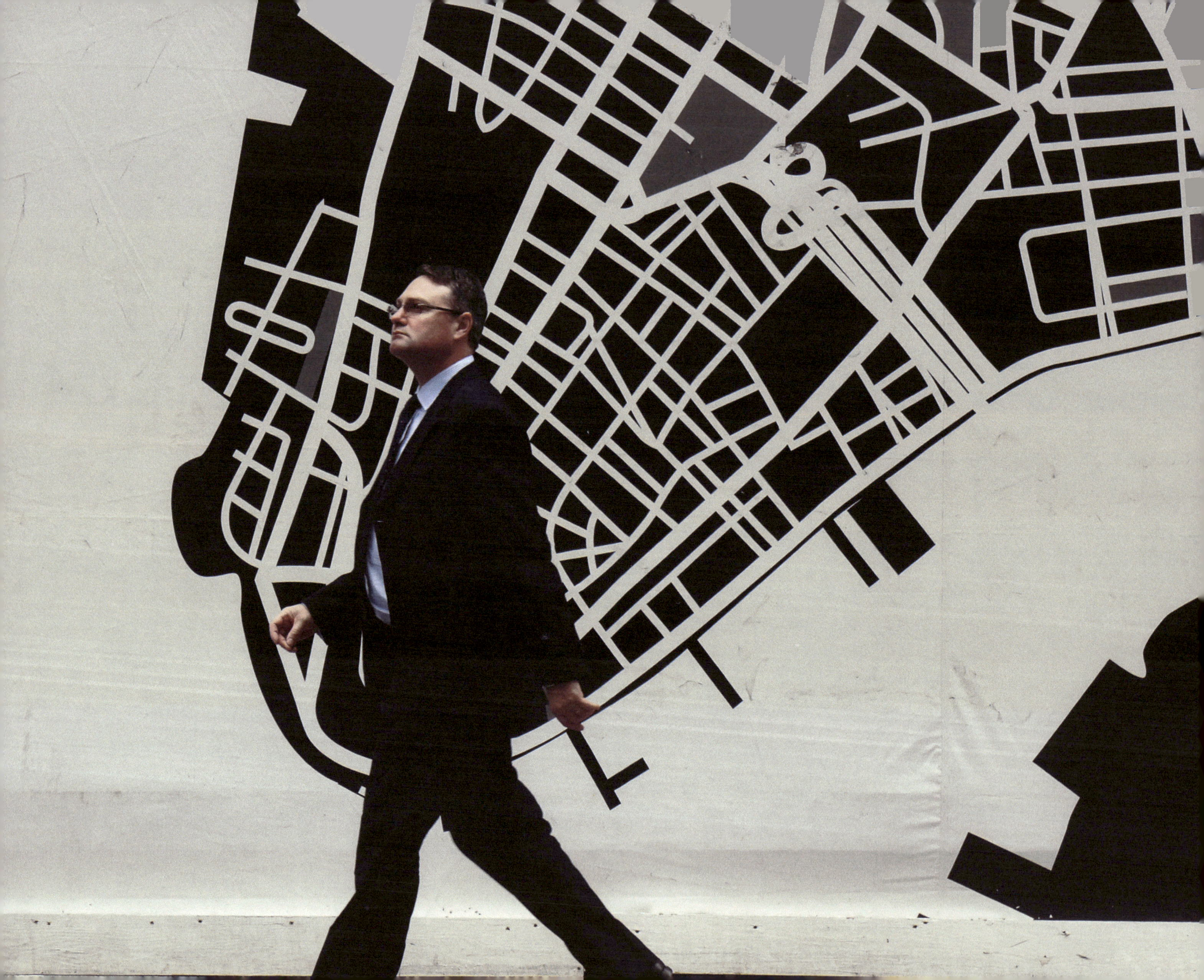

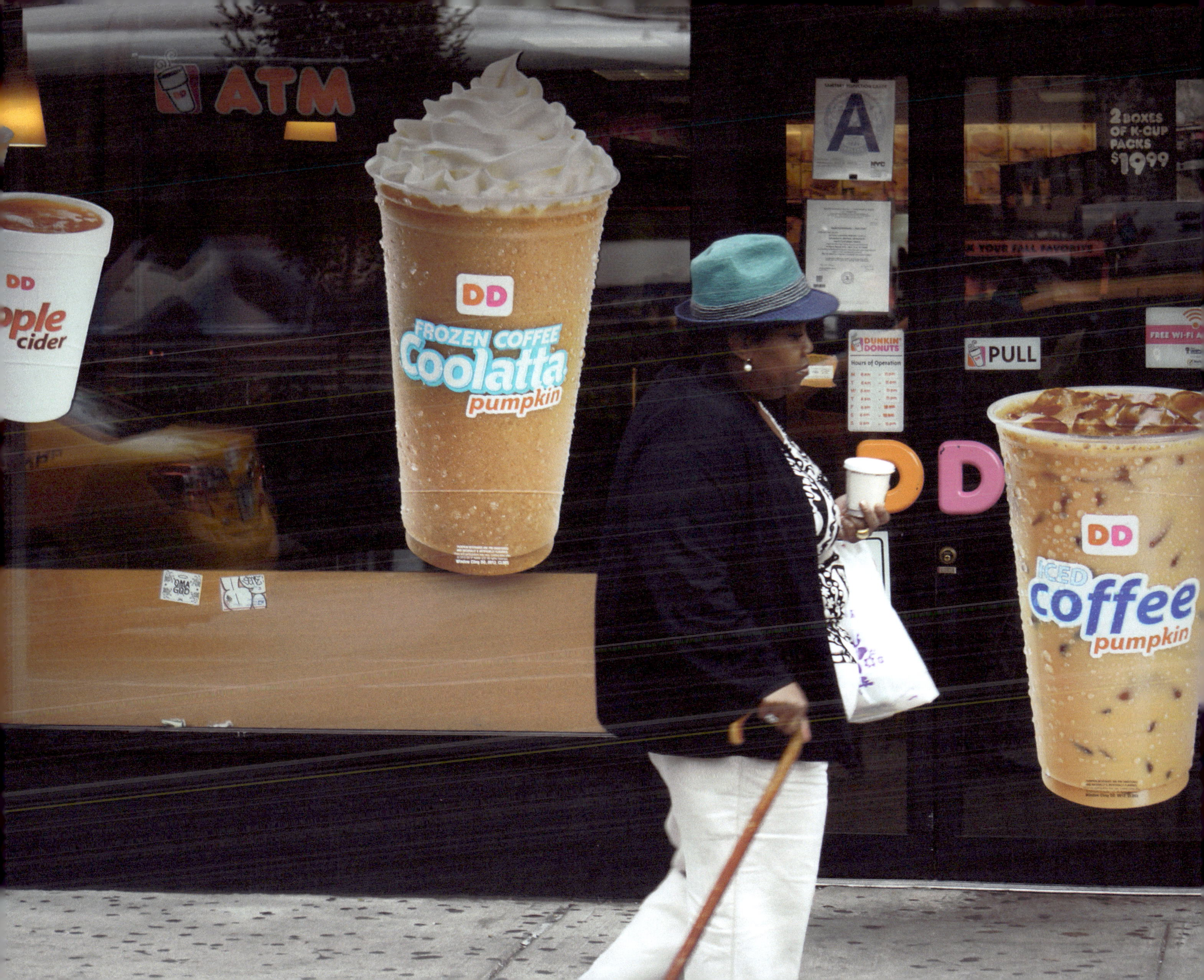
ATM
2 BOXES
OF K-CUP
PACKS
$19.99
DD
FROZEN COFFEE
Coolatta
pumpkin
DD
apple
cider
A
PULL
FREE WI-FI
DUNKIN'
DONUTS
Hours of Operation
DD
DD
ICED
Coffee
pumpkin

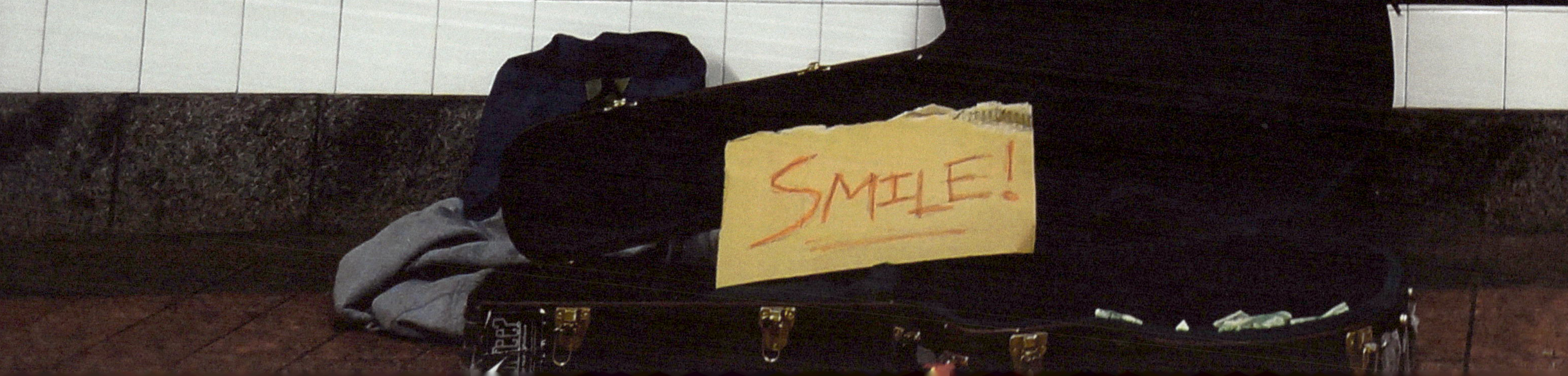

THE NEXT STEP IS JUST THE BEGINNING
SMILE!

KEEP WALKING.
JOHNNIE WALKER.

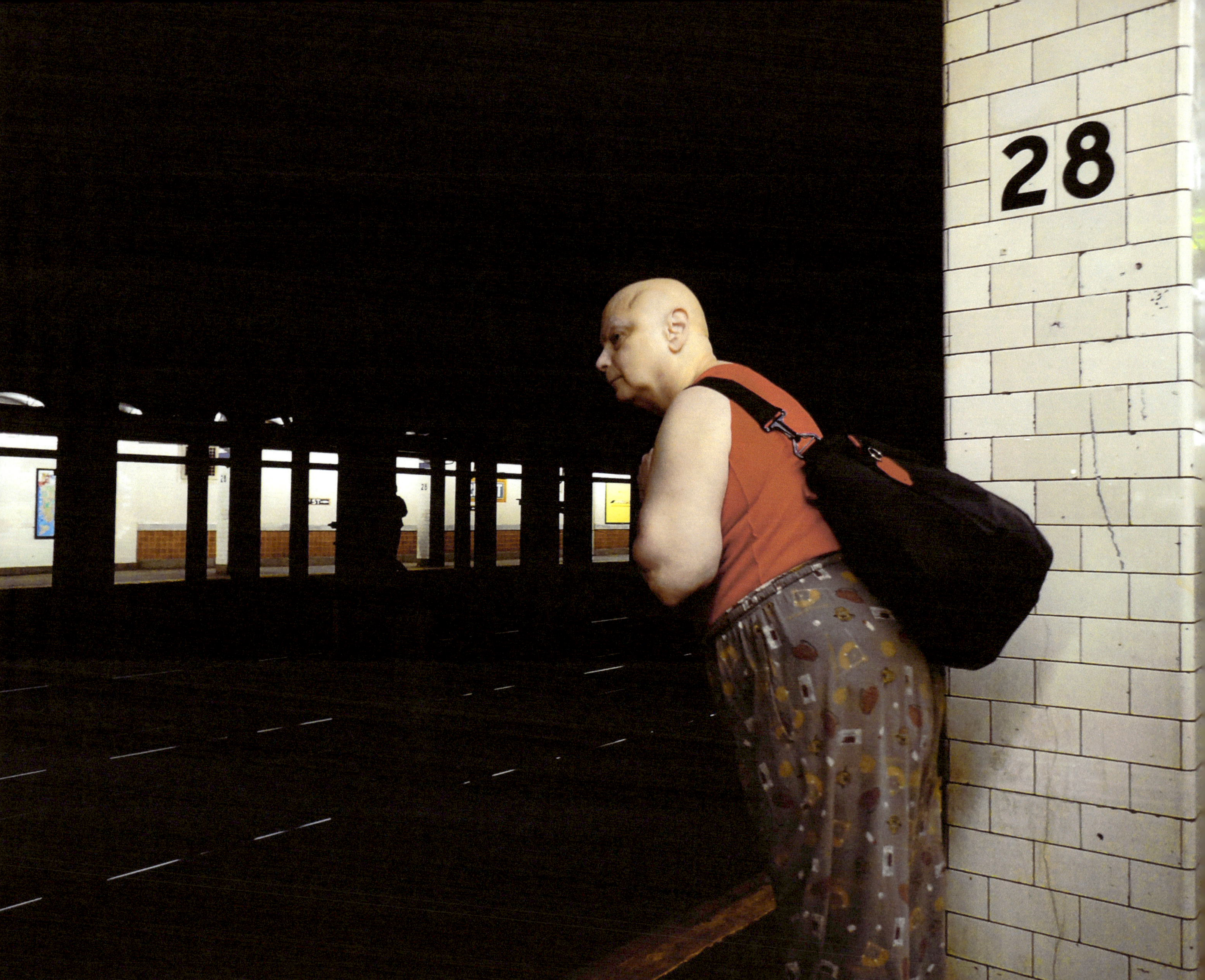

28

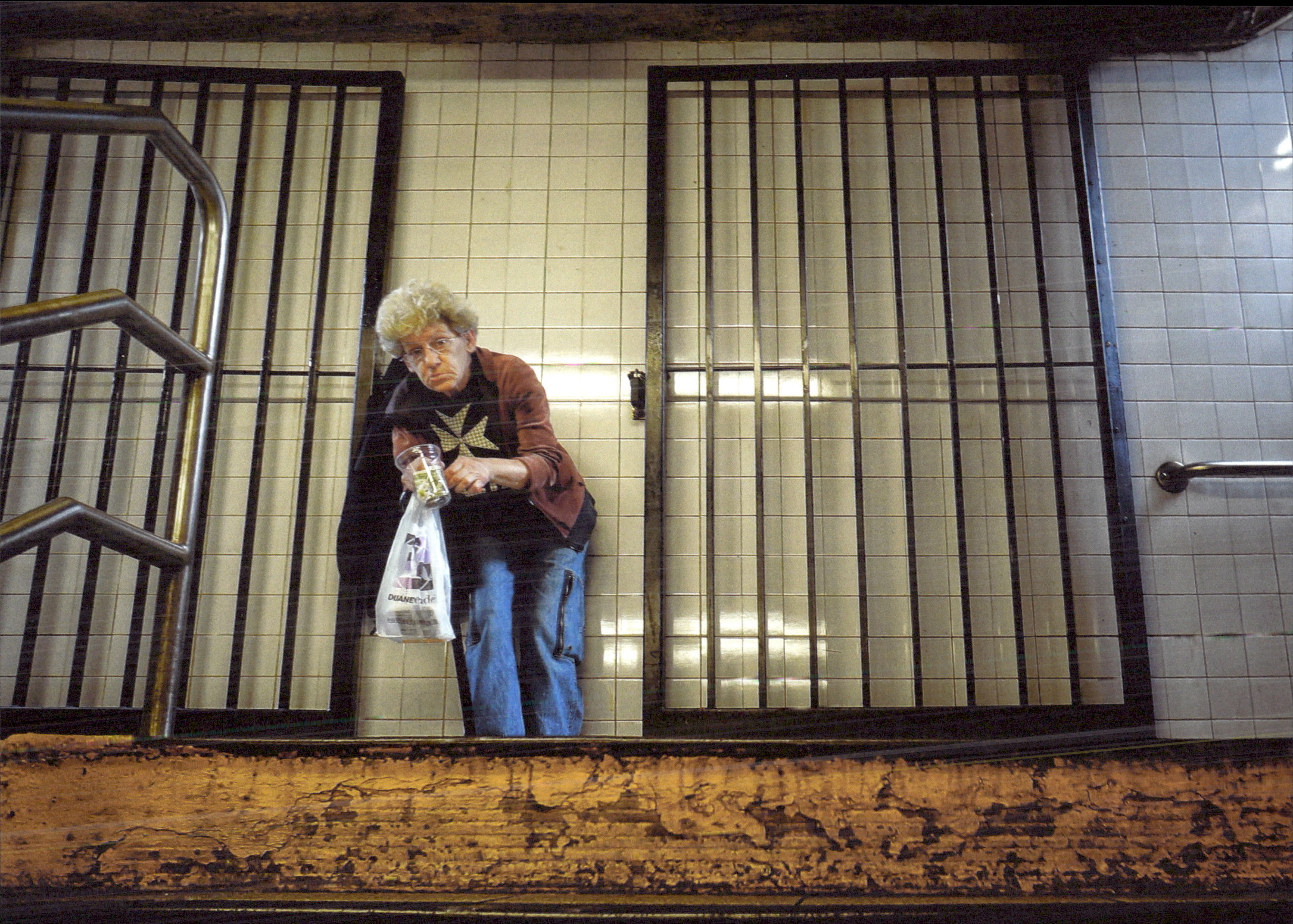

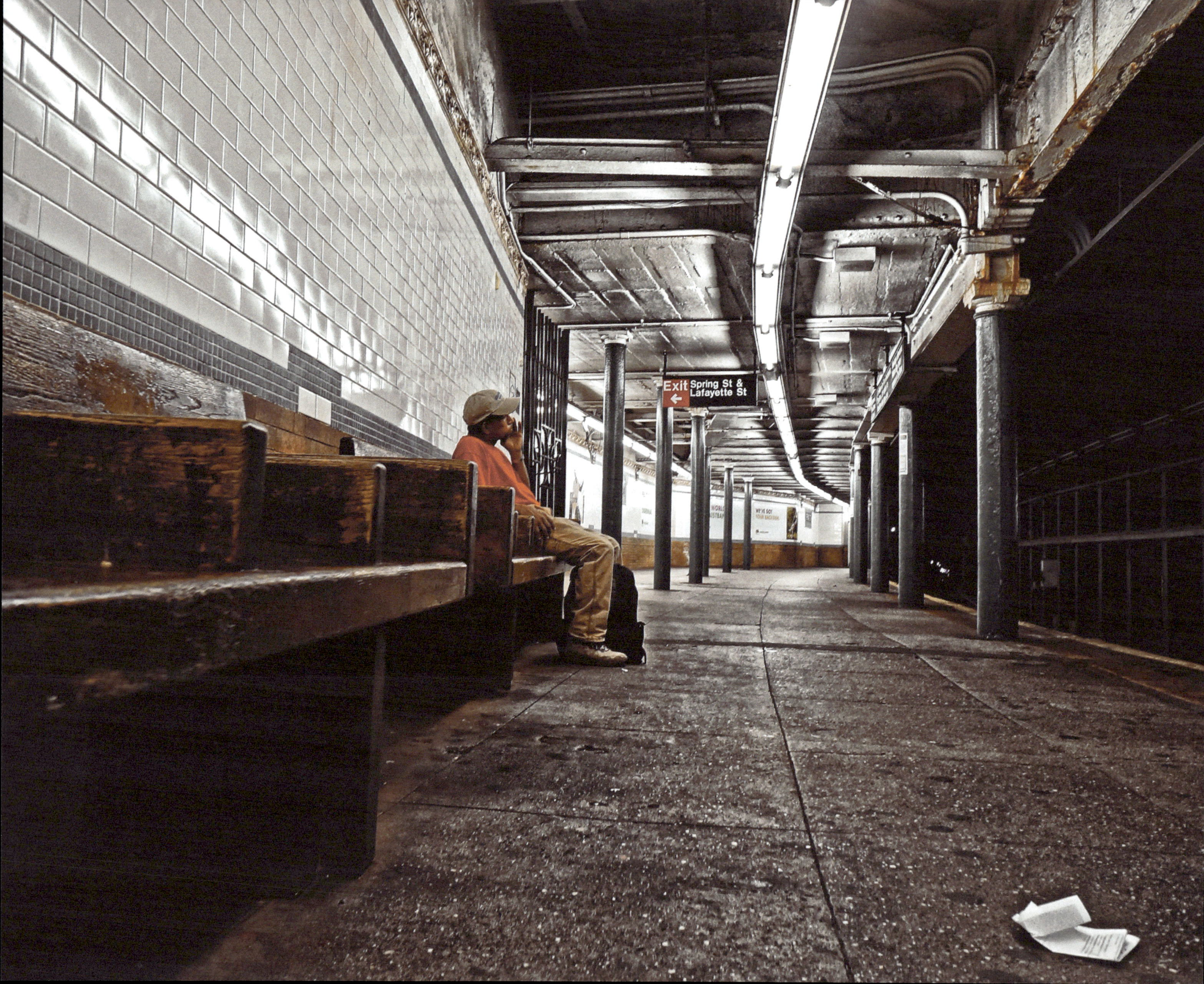

Exit Spring St &
Lafayette St

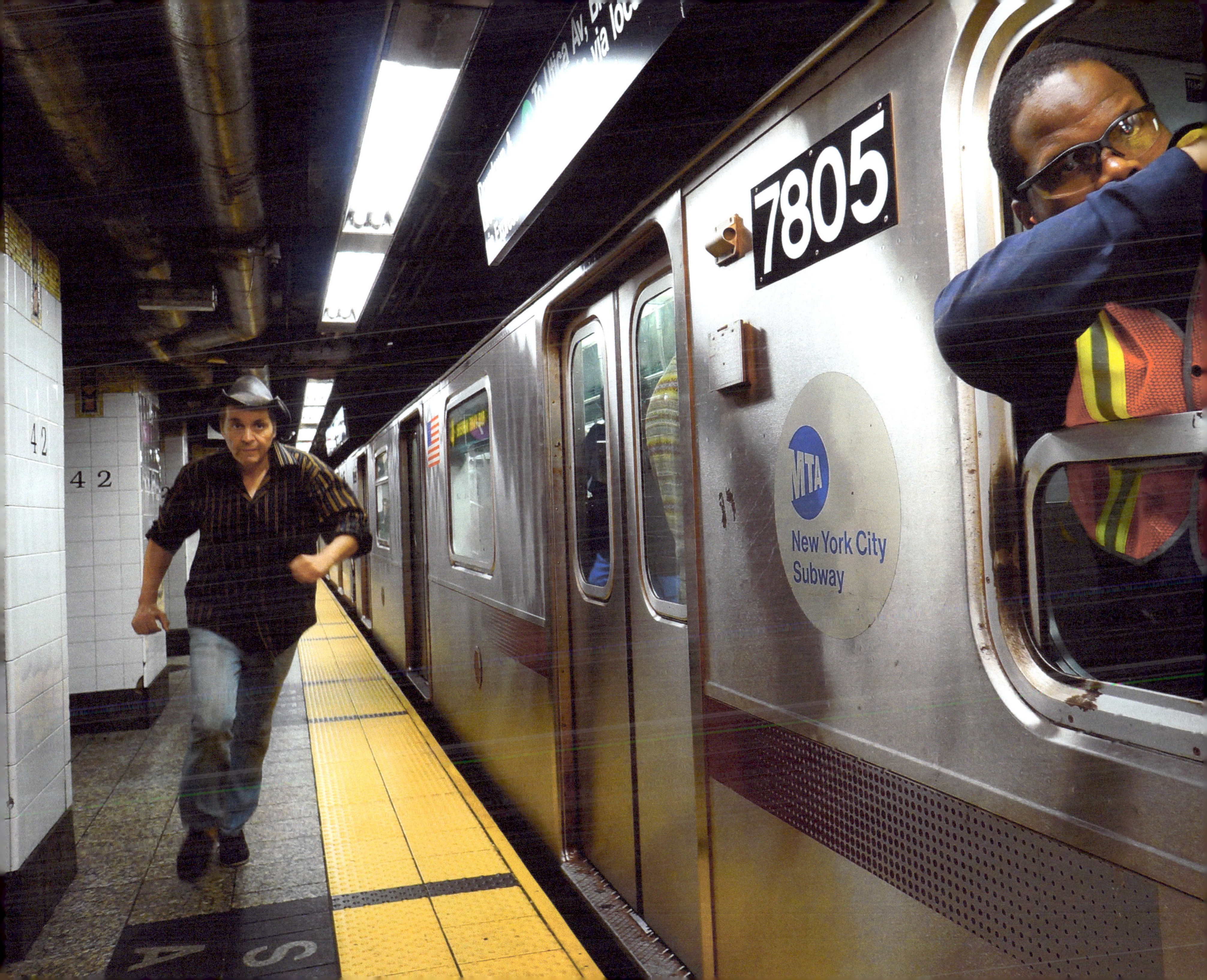

To Utica Av,
via loc
7805
MTA
New York City
Subway
42
42

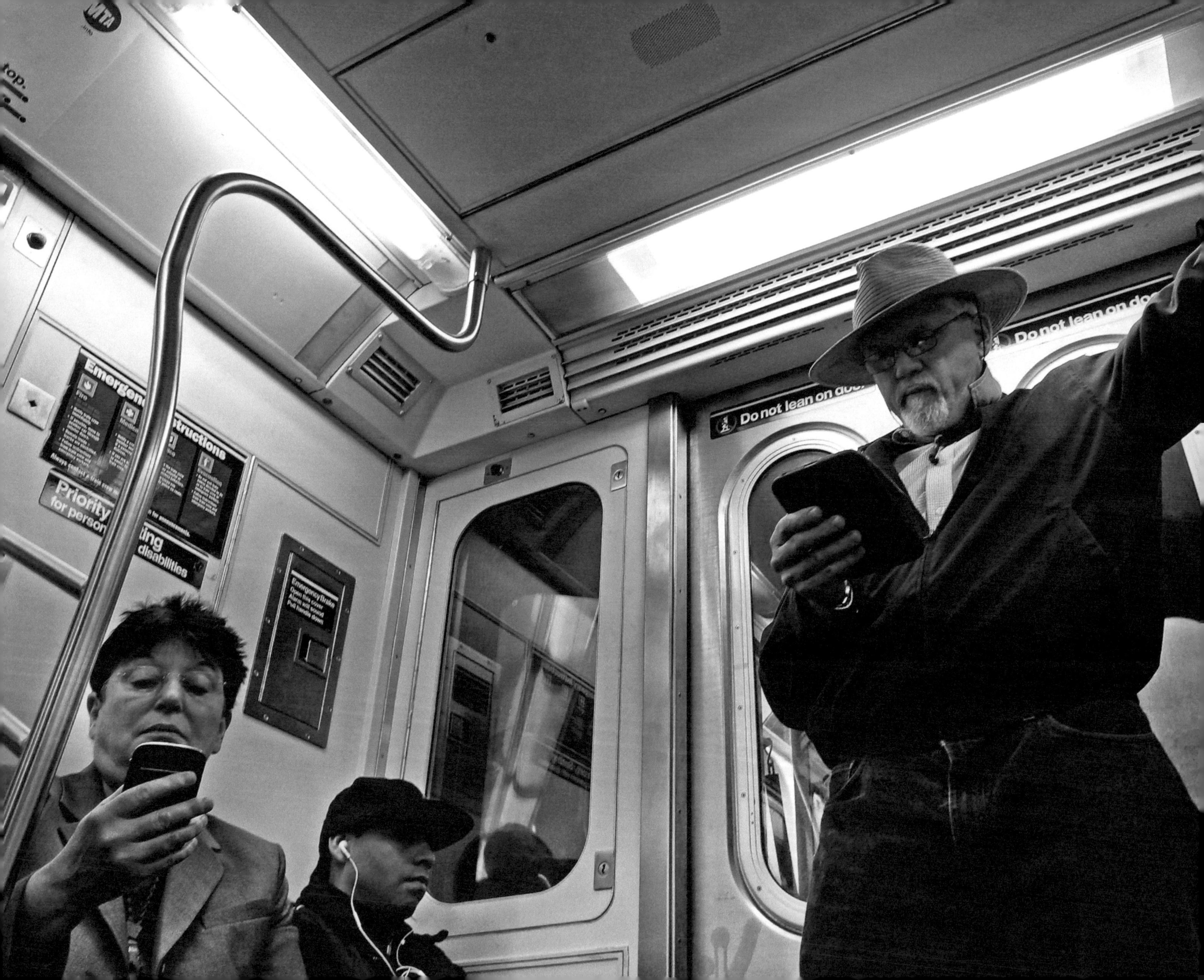
Do not lean on door
Do not lean on door
Emergency
Instructions
Priority
for person
disabilities
Emergency Brake
Open this cover
Alarm will sound
Pull handle down

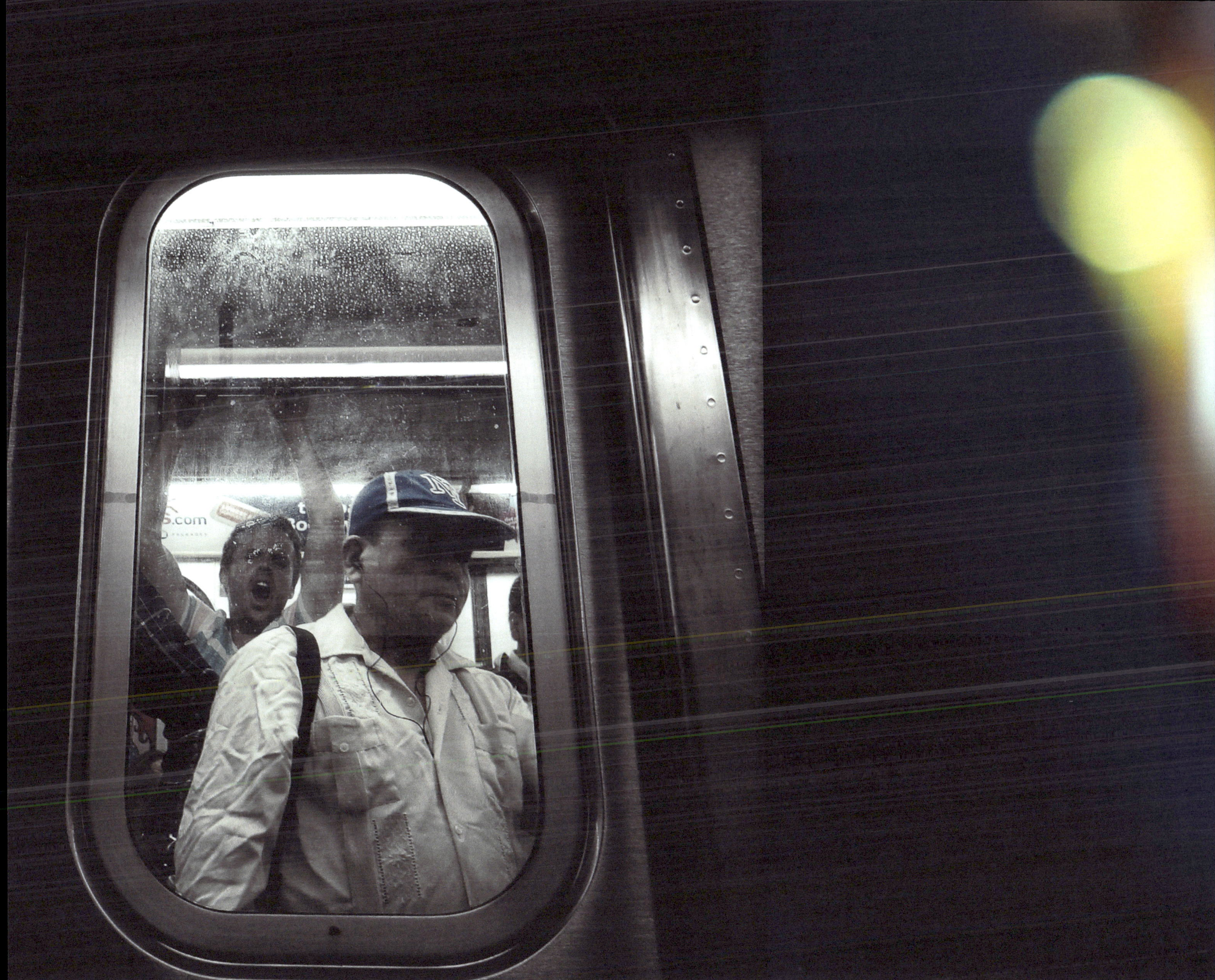

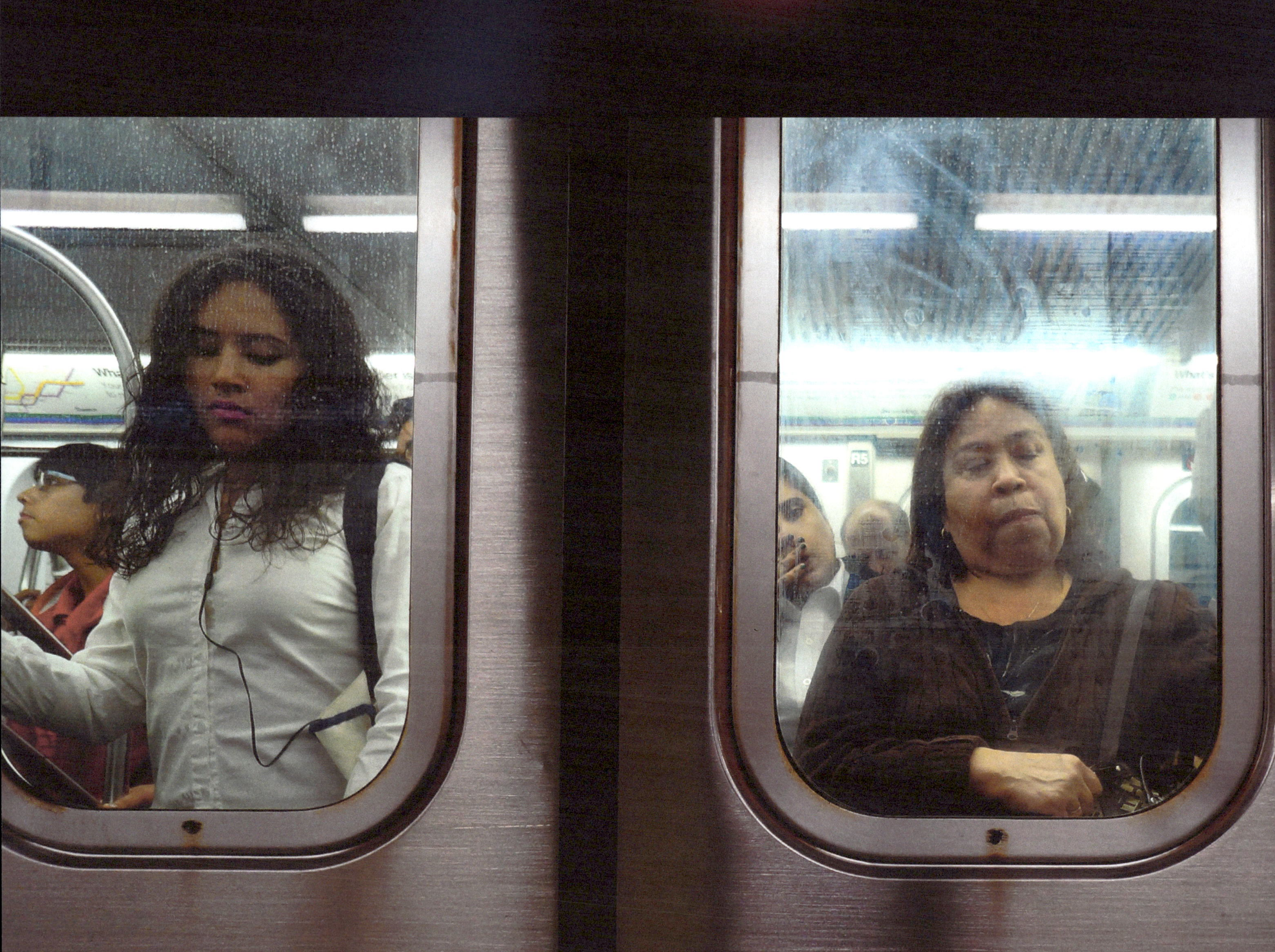

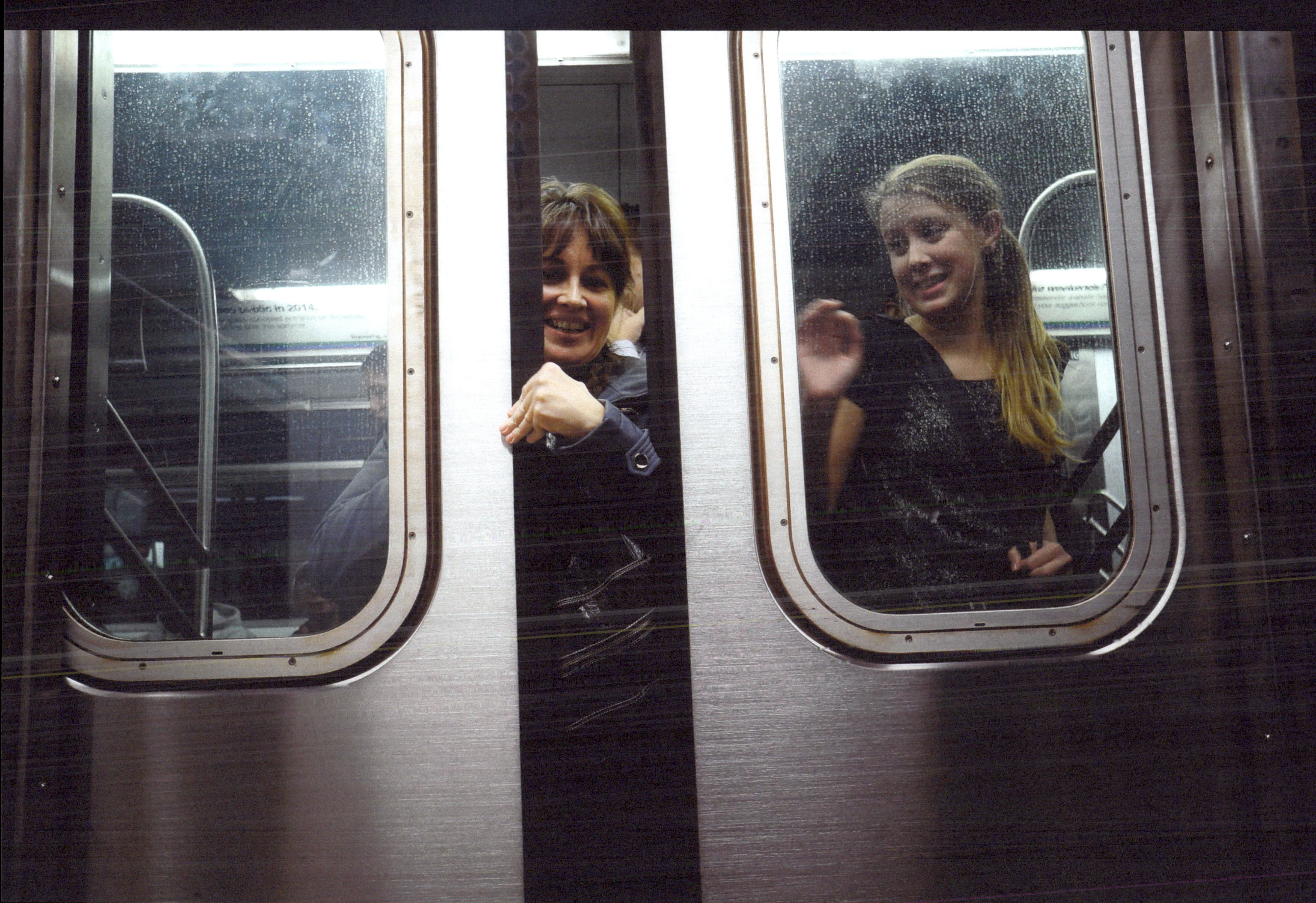

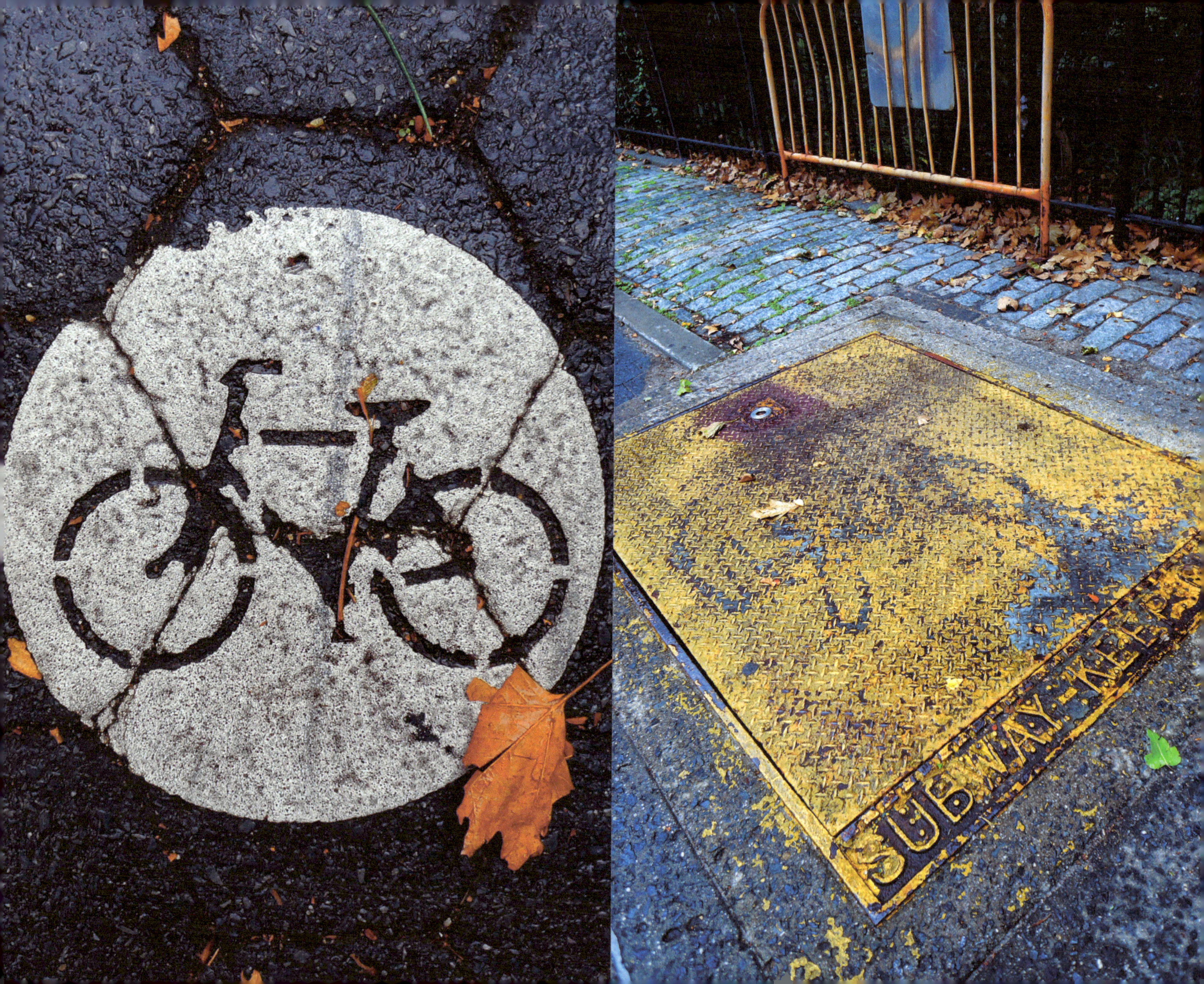

SUBWAY · KEEP

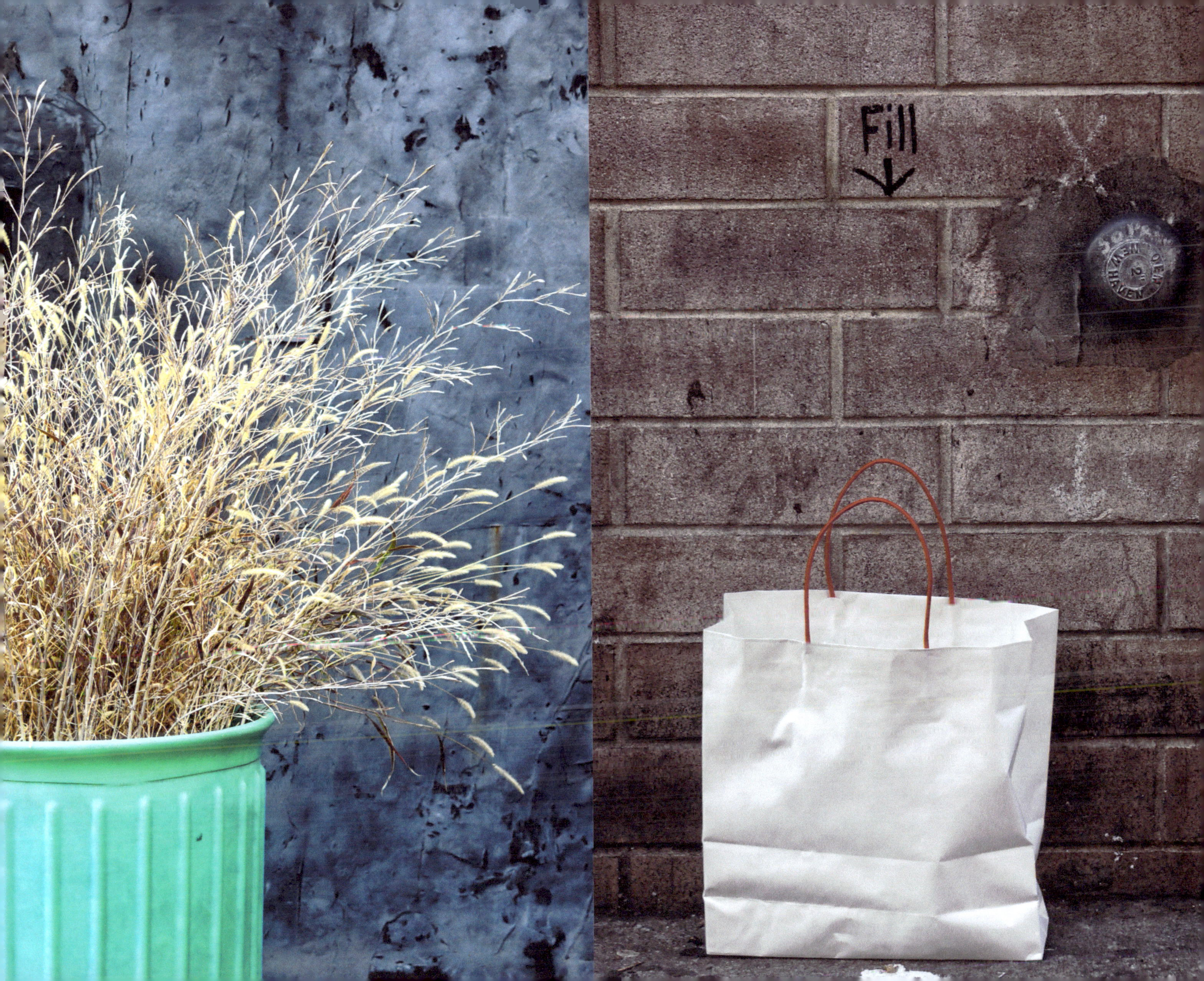

Fill

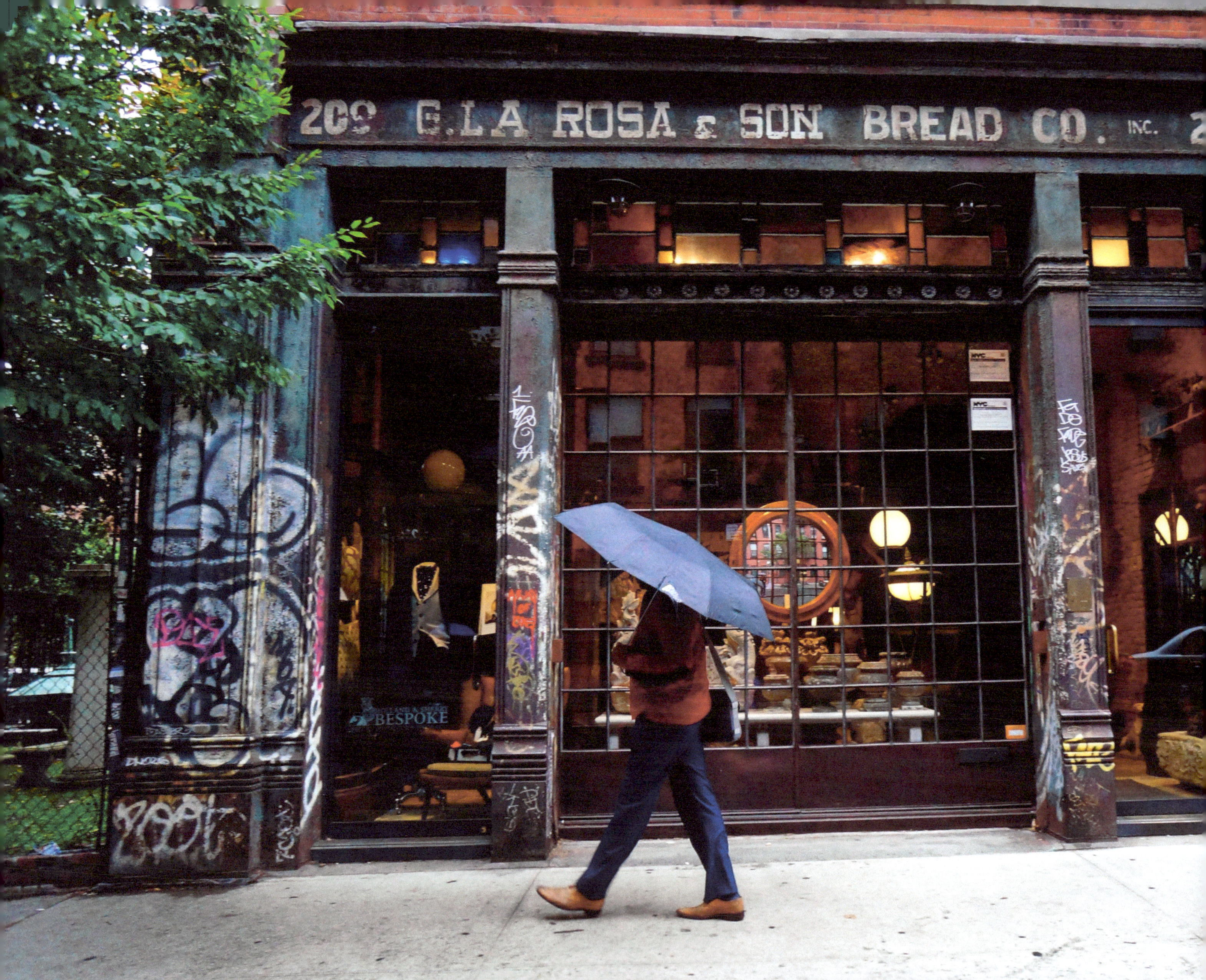
209   G. LA ROSA & SON BREAD CO. INC.
BESPOKE

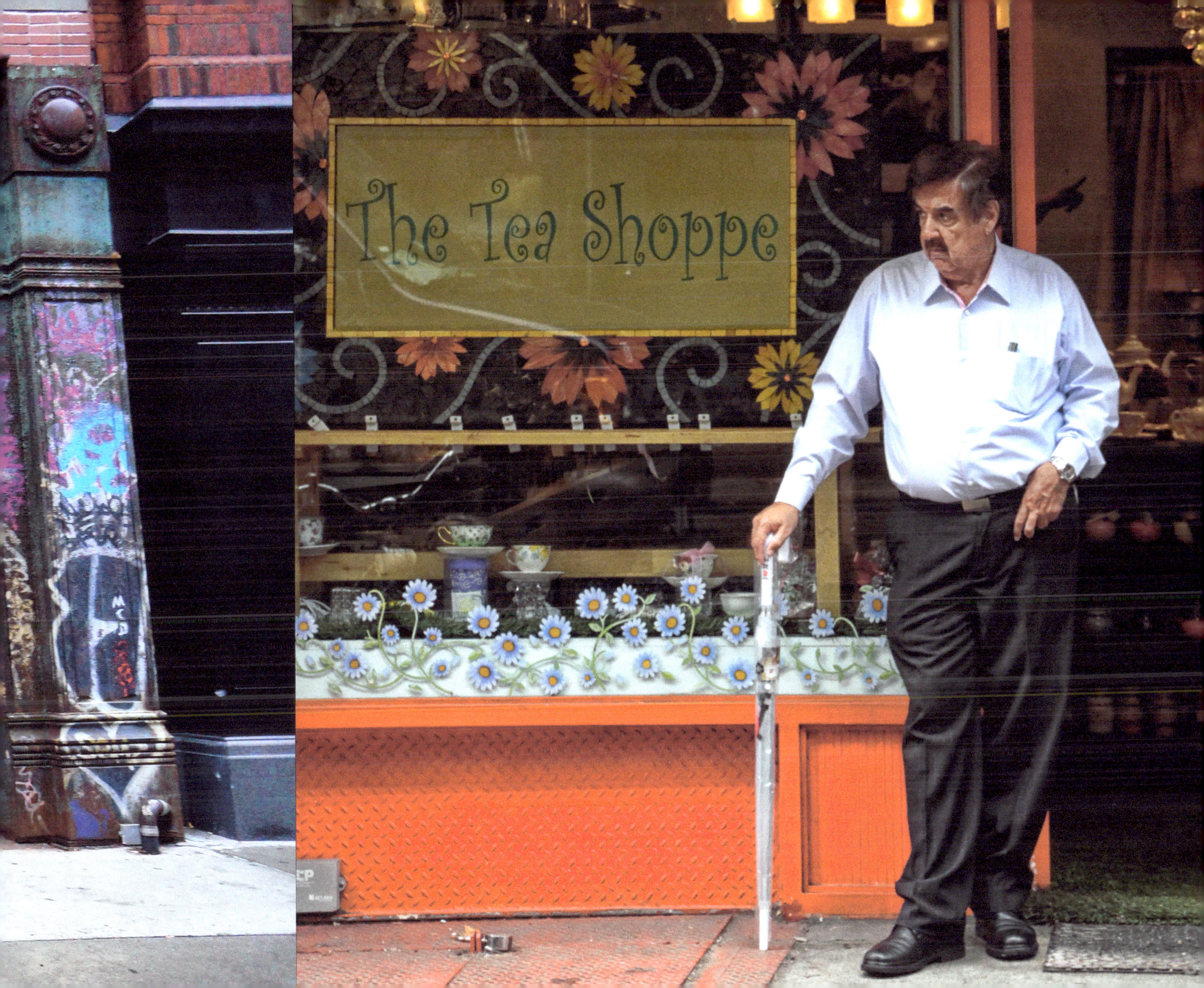
The Tea Shoppe

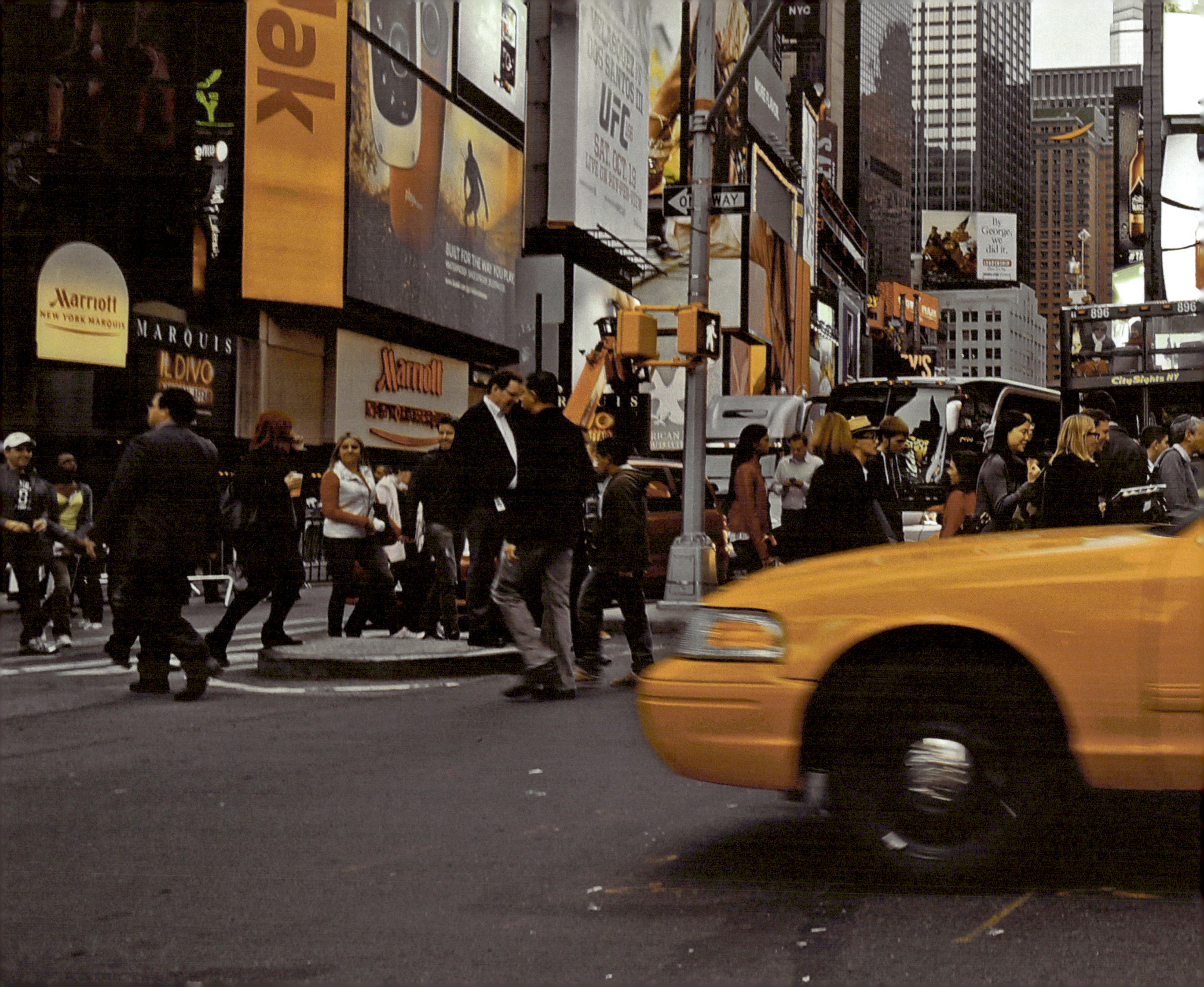
Marriott
NEW YORK MARQUIS
MARQUIS
IL DIVO
Marriott
UFC
SAT. OCT. 19
LIVE ON PAY-PER-VIEW
BUILT FOR THE WAY YOU PLAY
By George,
we
did it.
ONE WAY
NYC
896
896
CitySights NY

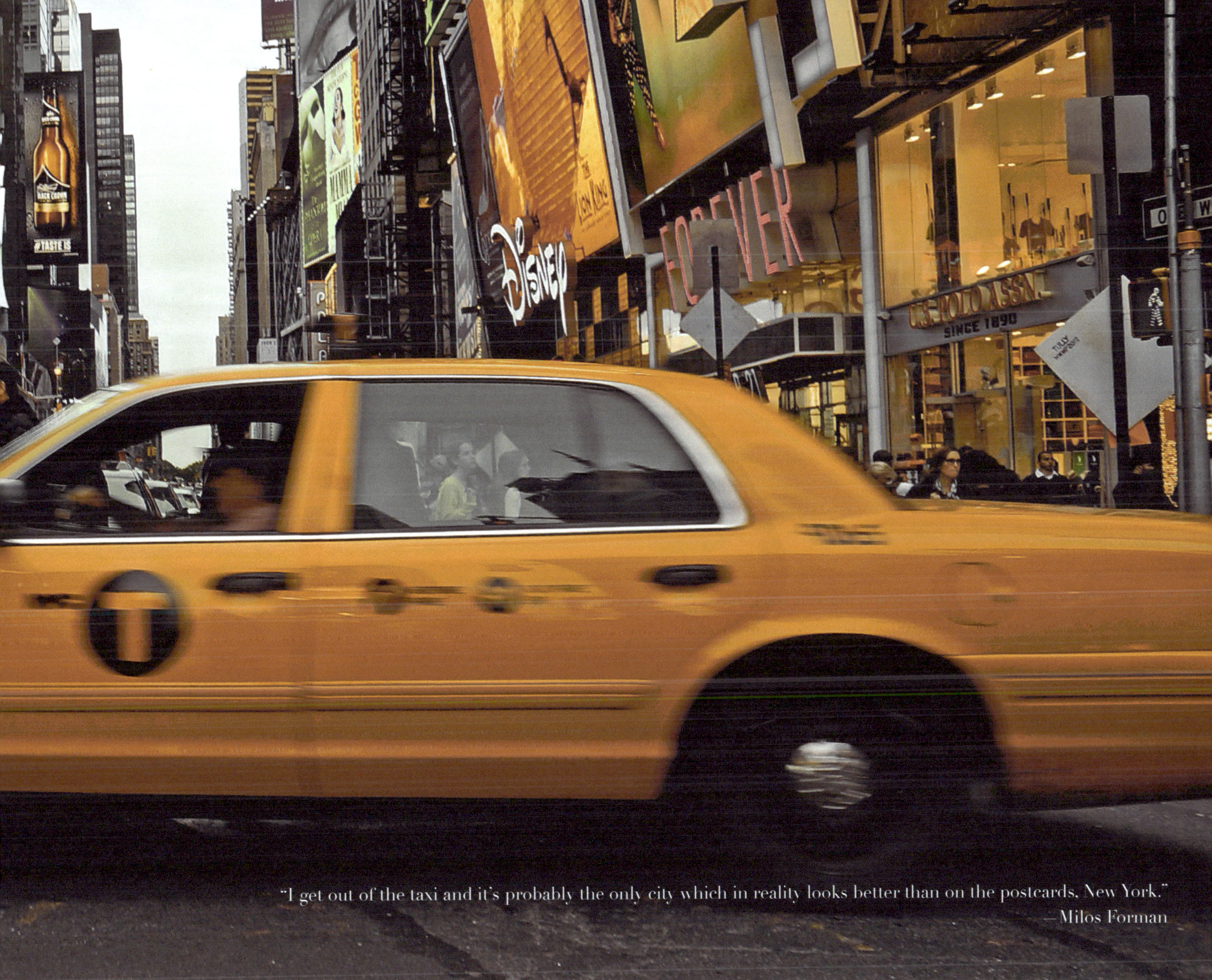

"I get out of the taxi and it's probably the only city which in reality looks better than on the postcards. New York."
— Milos Forman

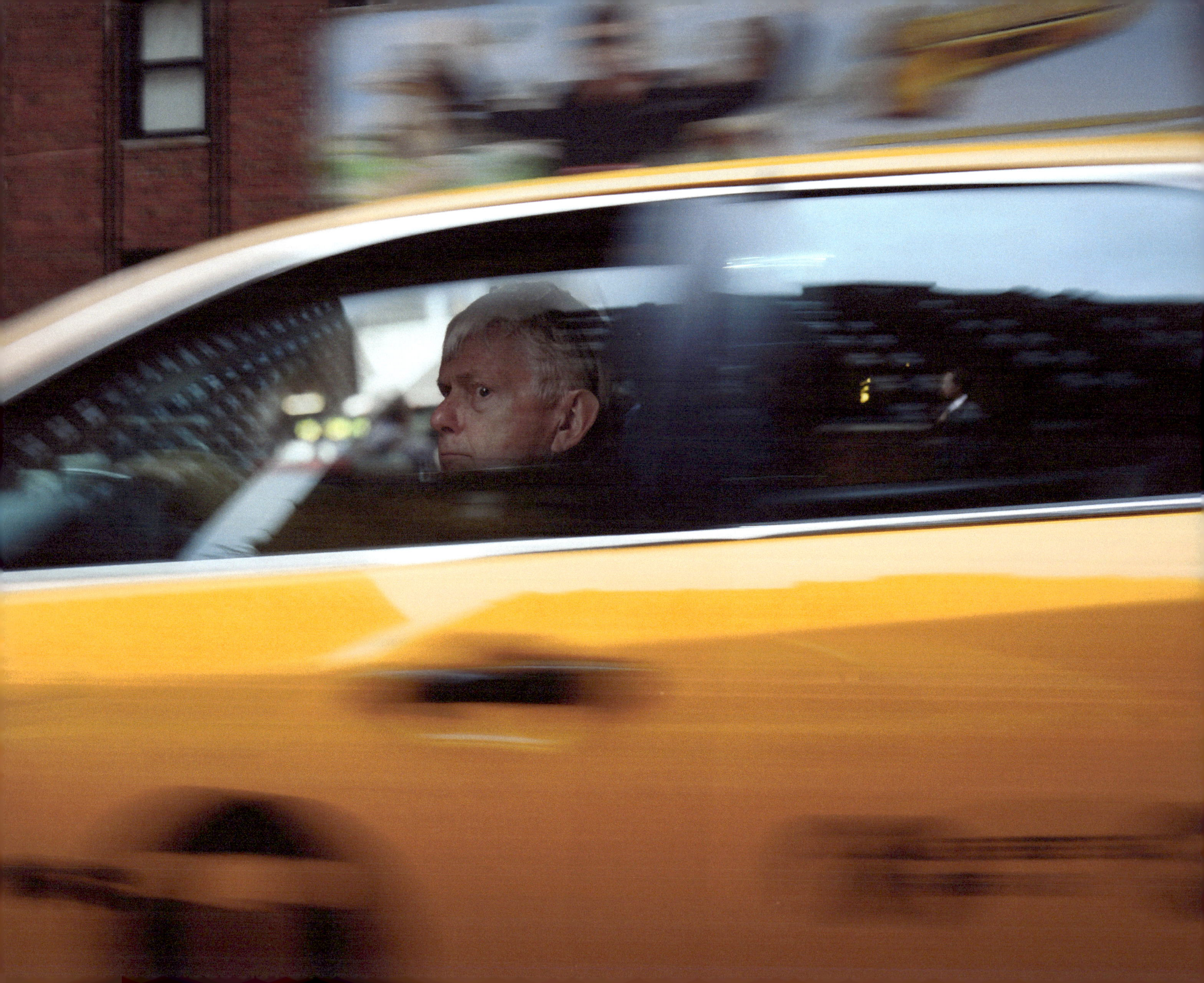

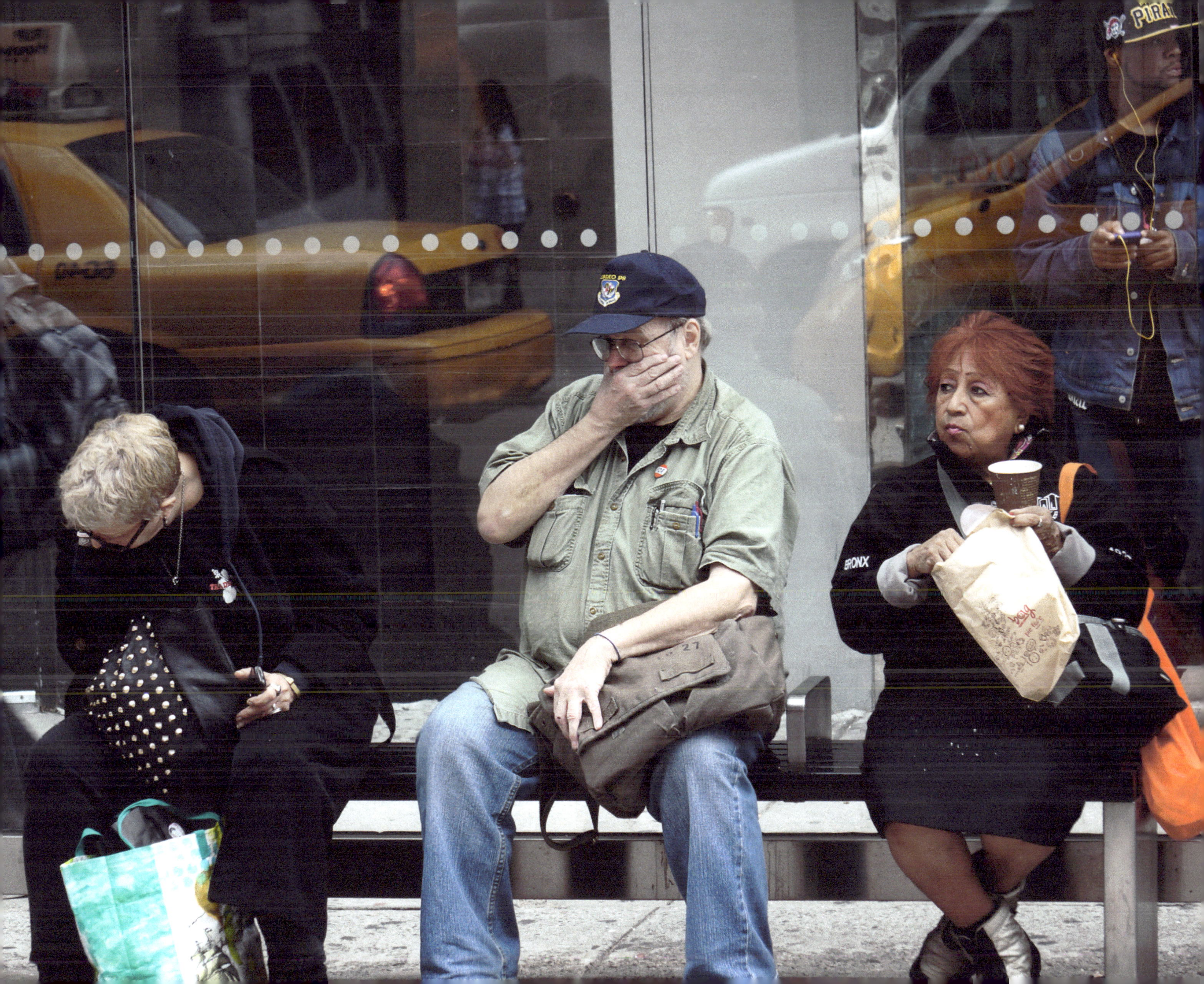

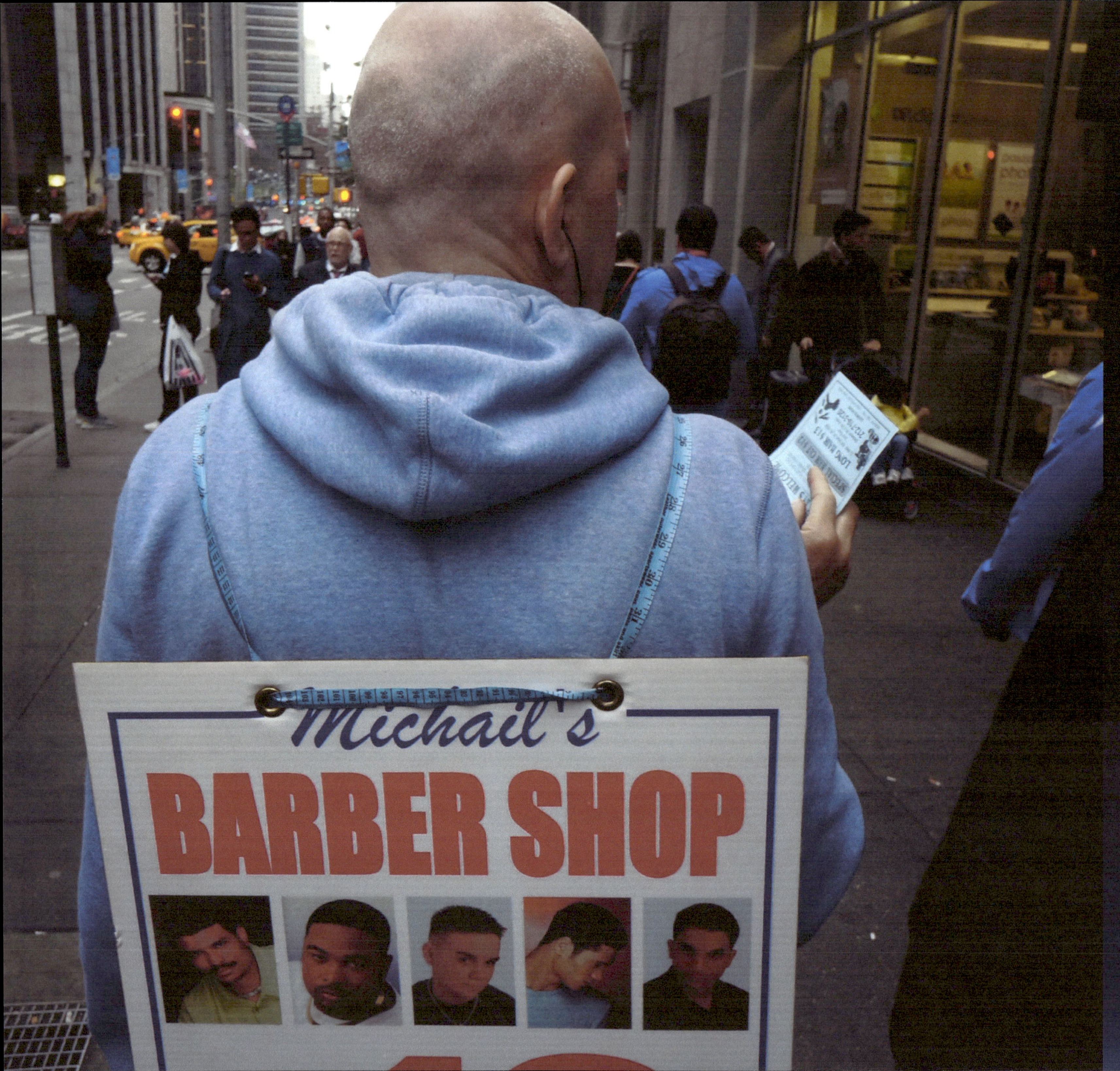

Michail's
BARBER SHOP

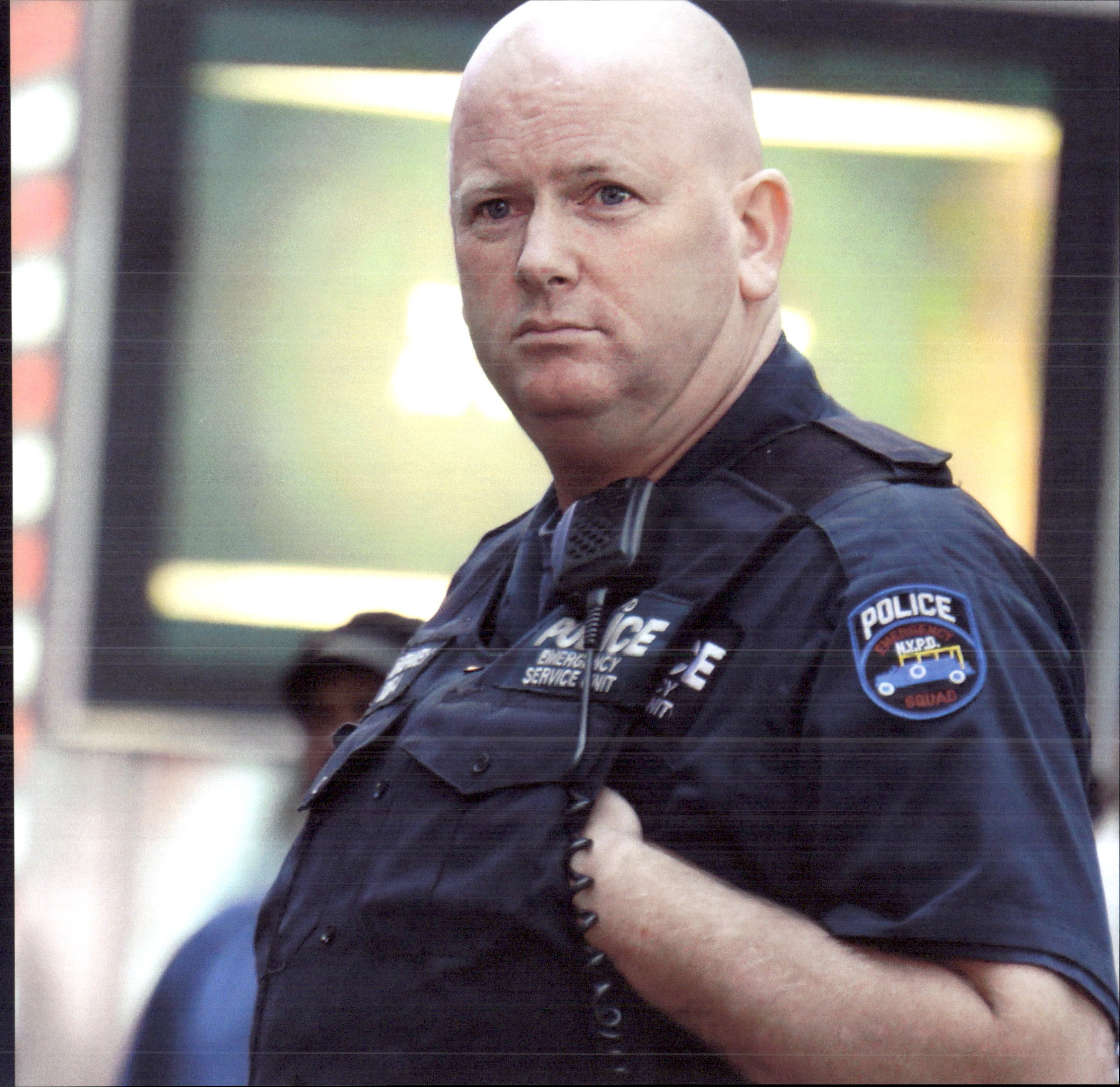
POLICE
EMERGENCY
SERVICE UNIT
POLICE
EMERGENCY
N.Y.P.D.
SQUAD

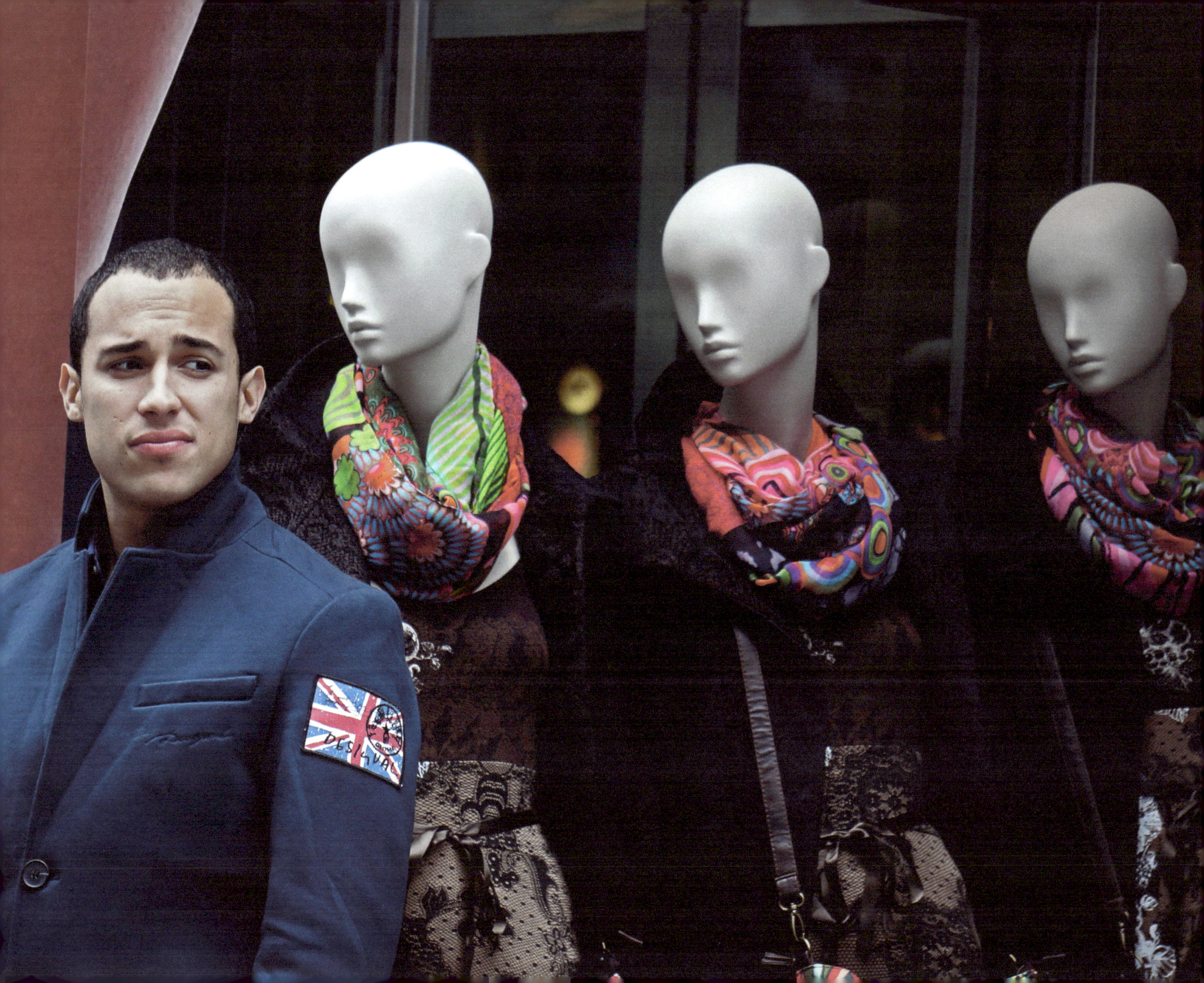

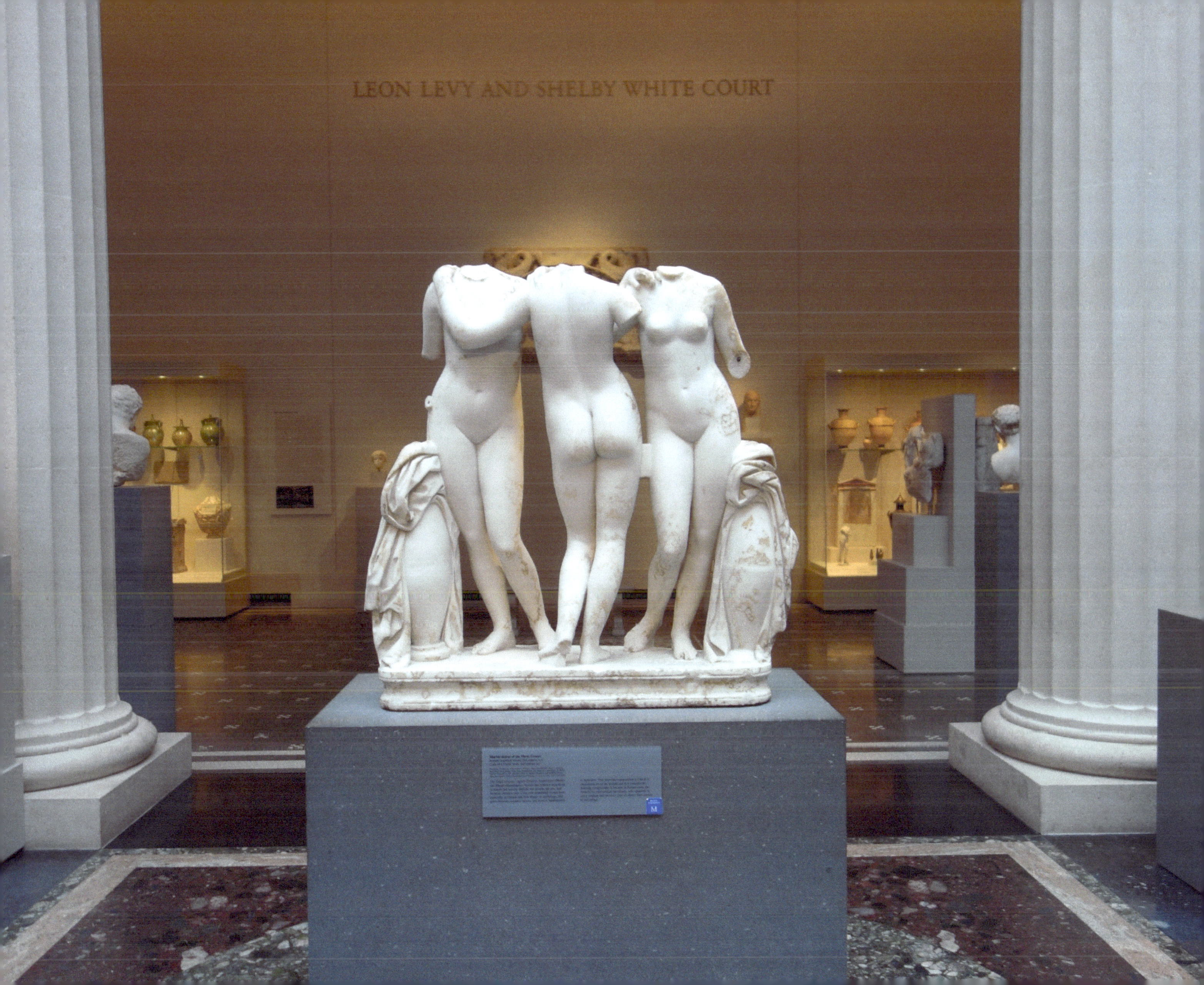

LEON LEVY AND SHELBY WHITE COURT

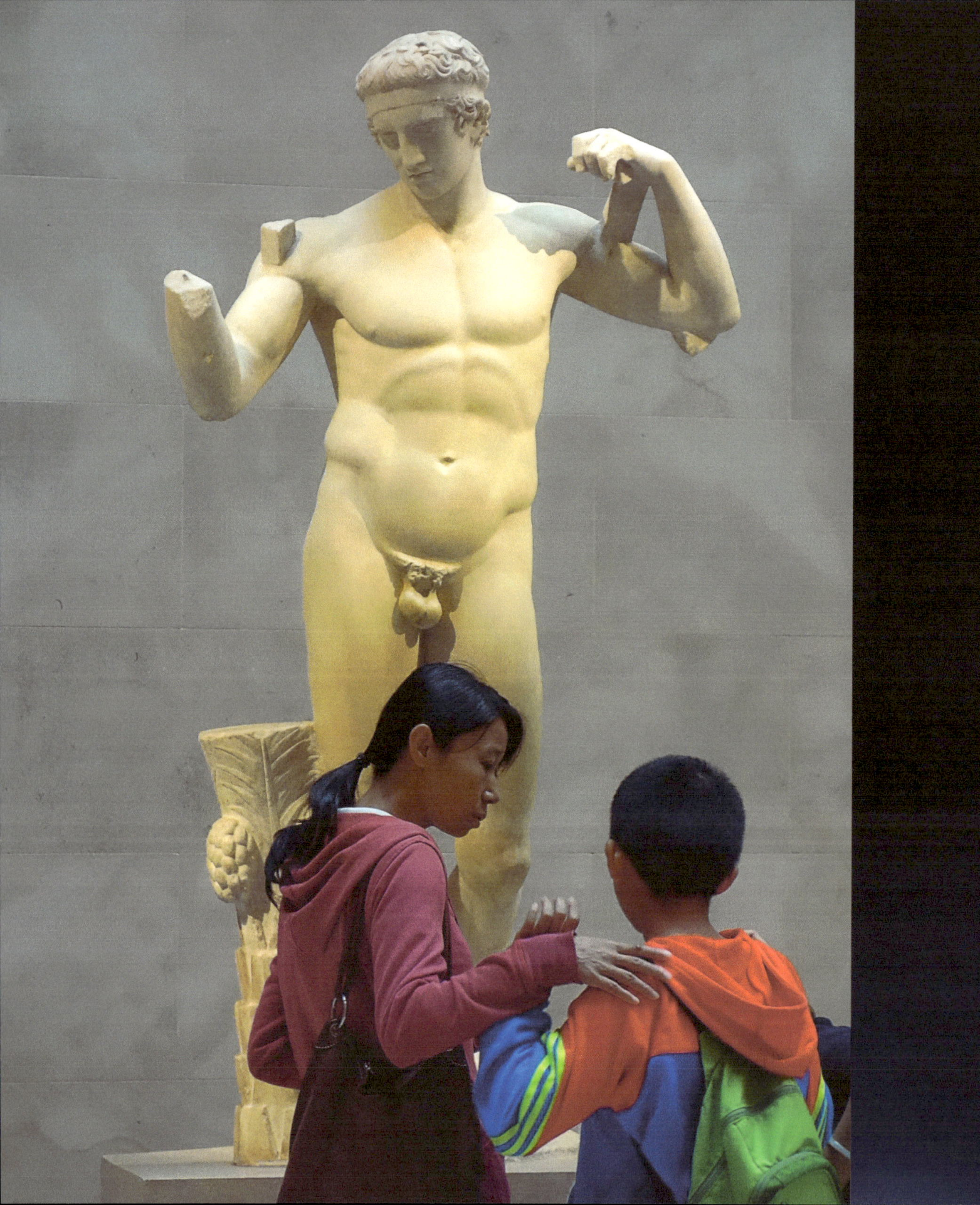

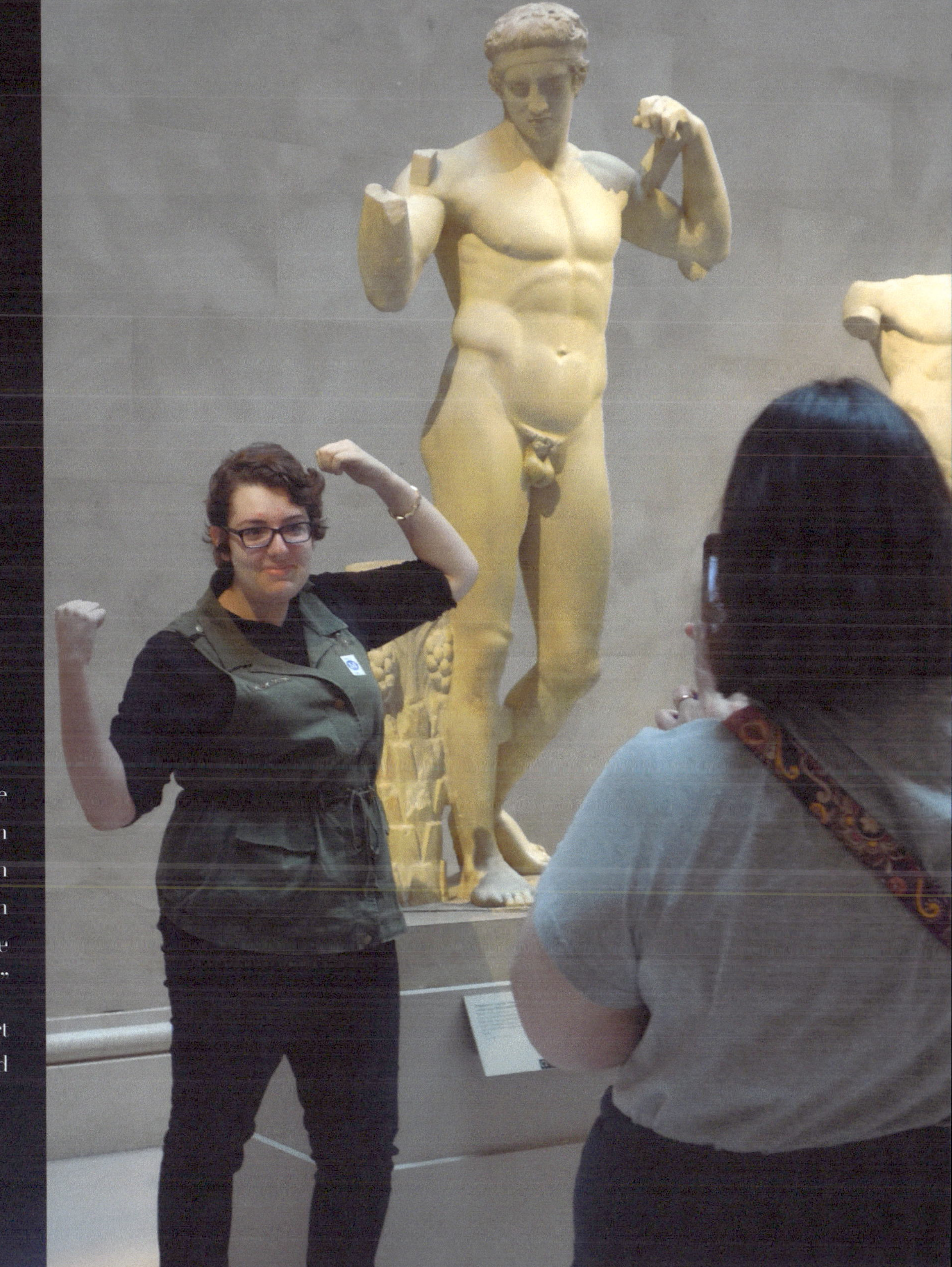
"There is more
sophistication
and less sense in
New York than
anywhere else
on the globe."

—Elbert
Hubbard

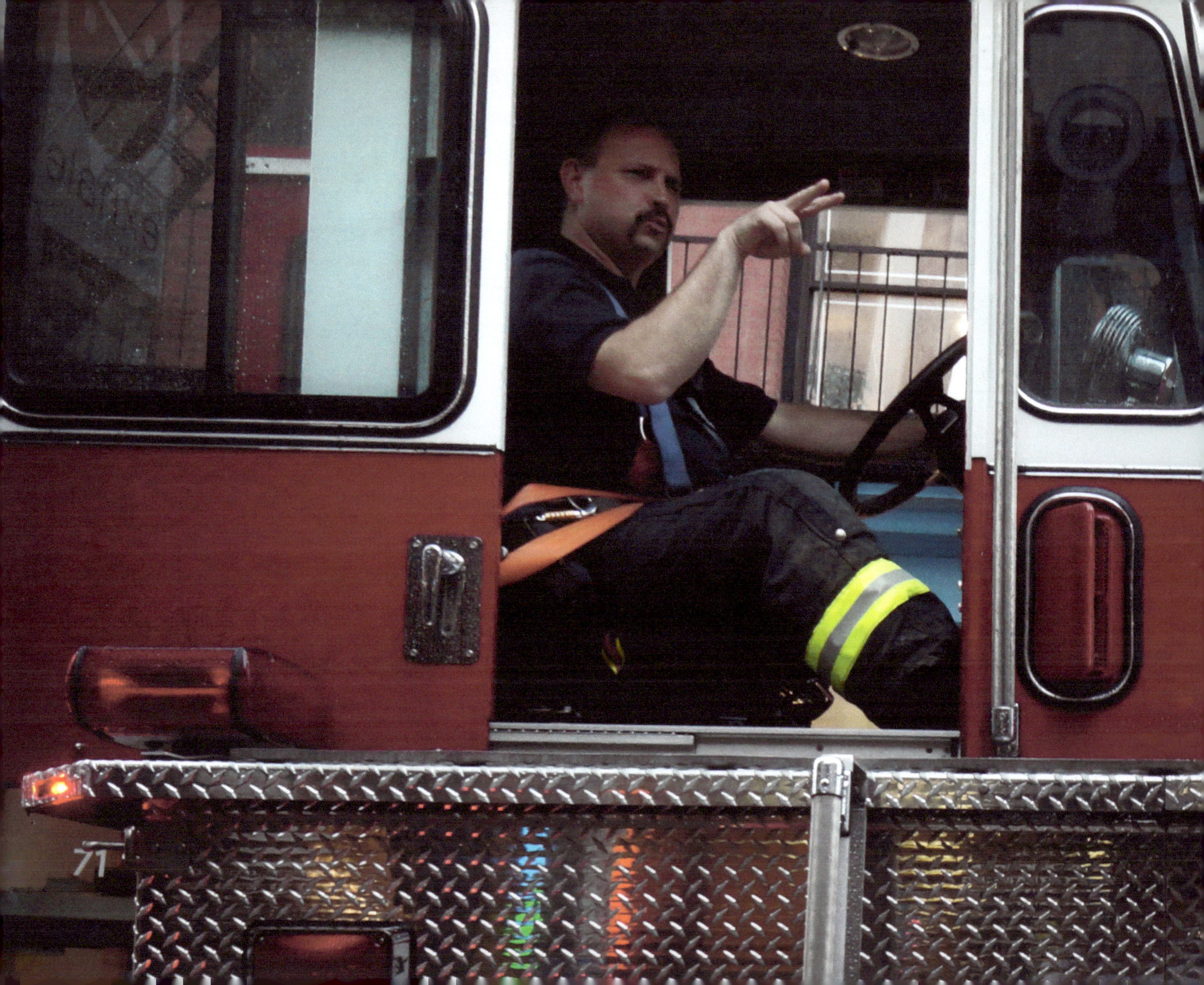

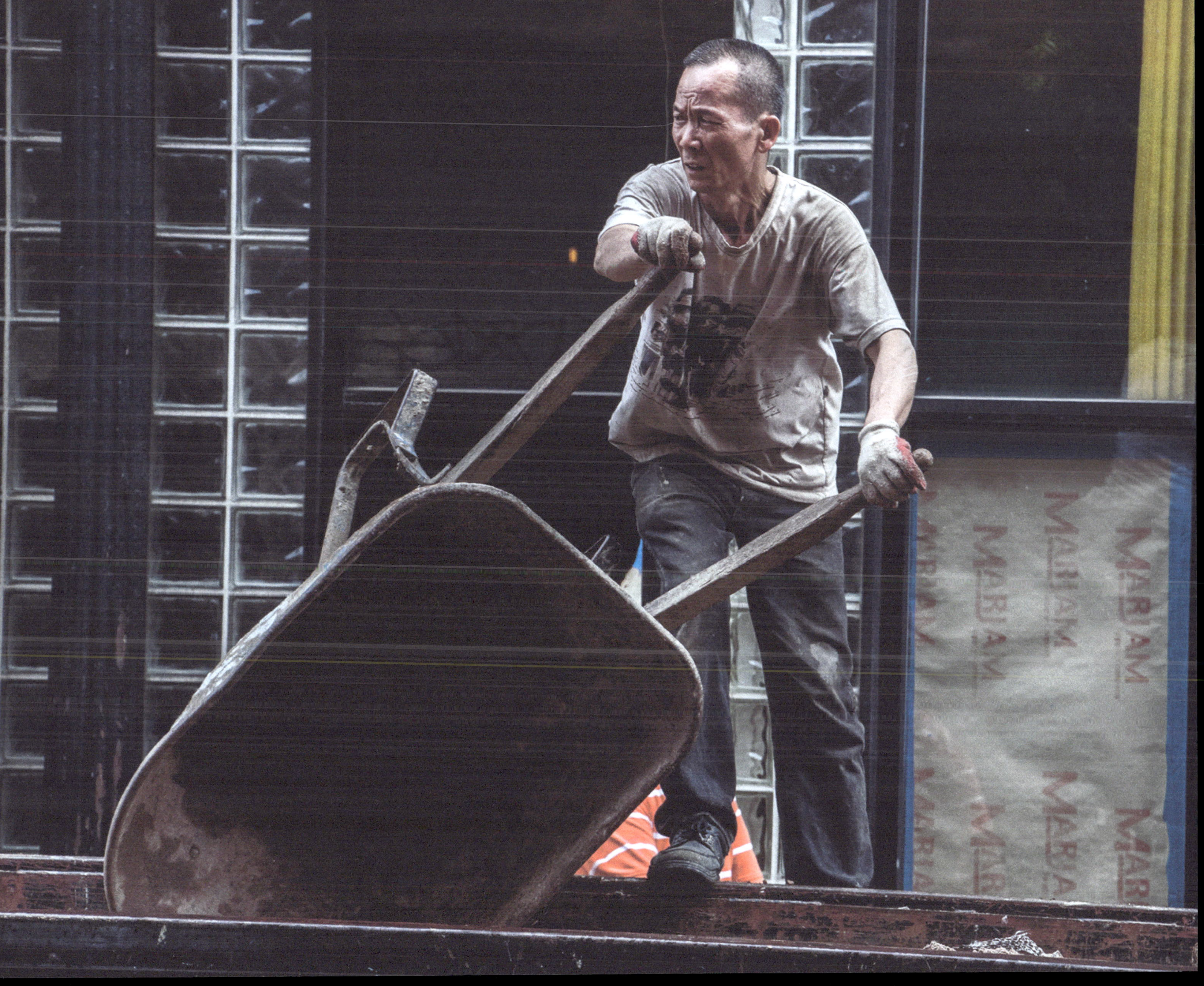

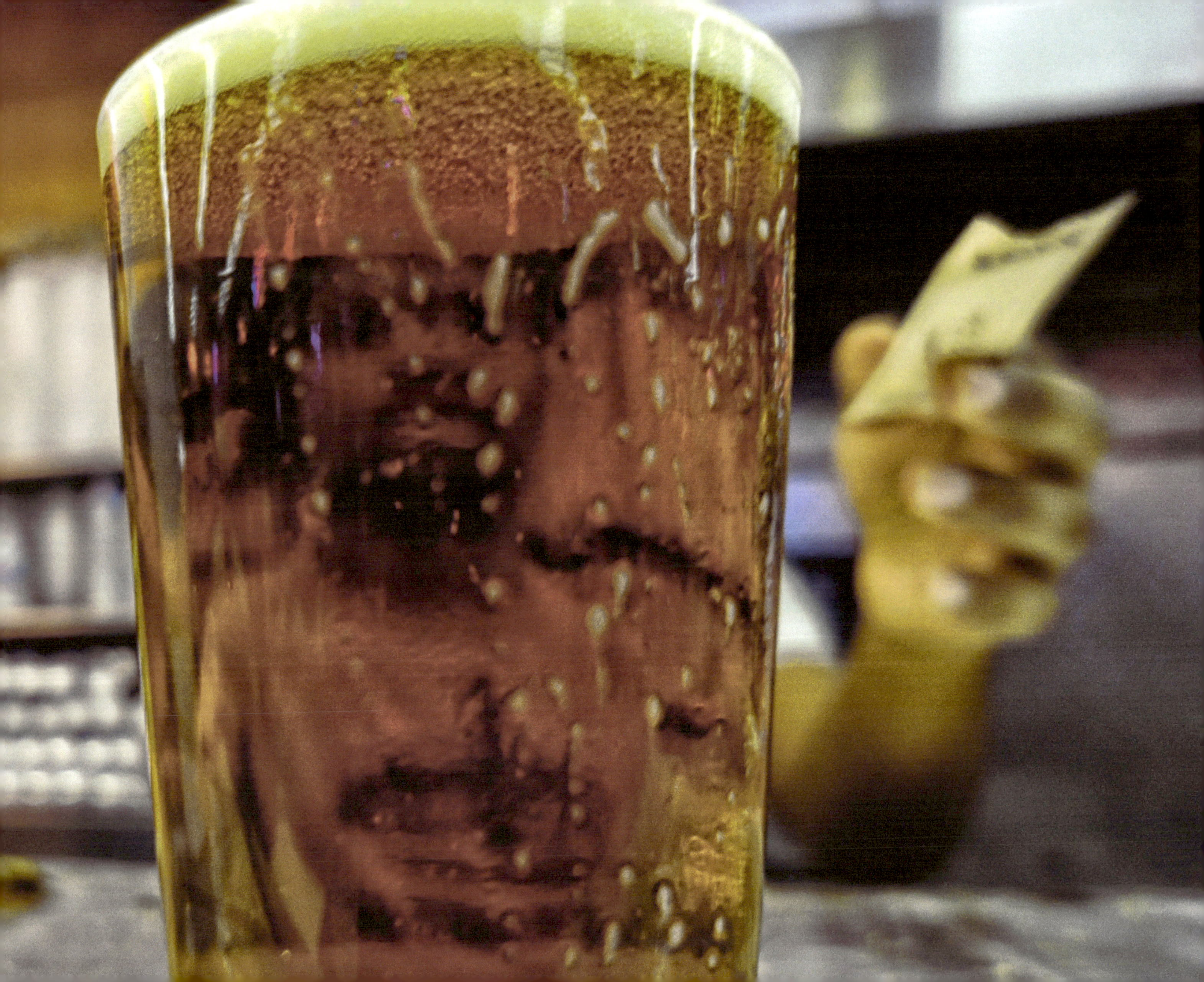

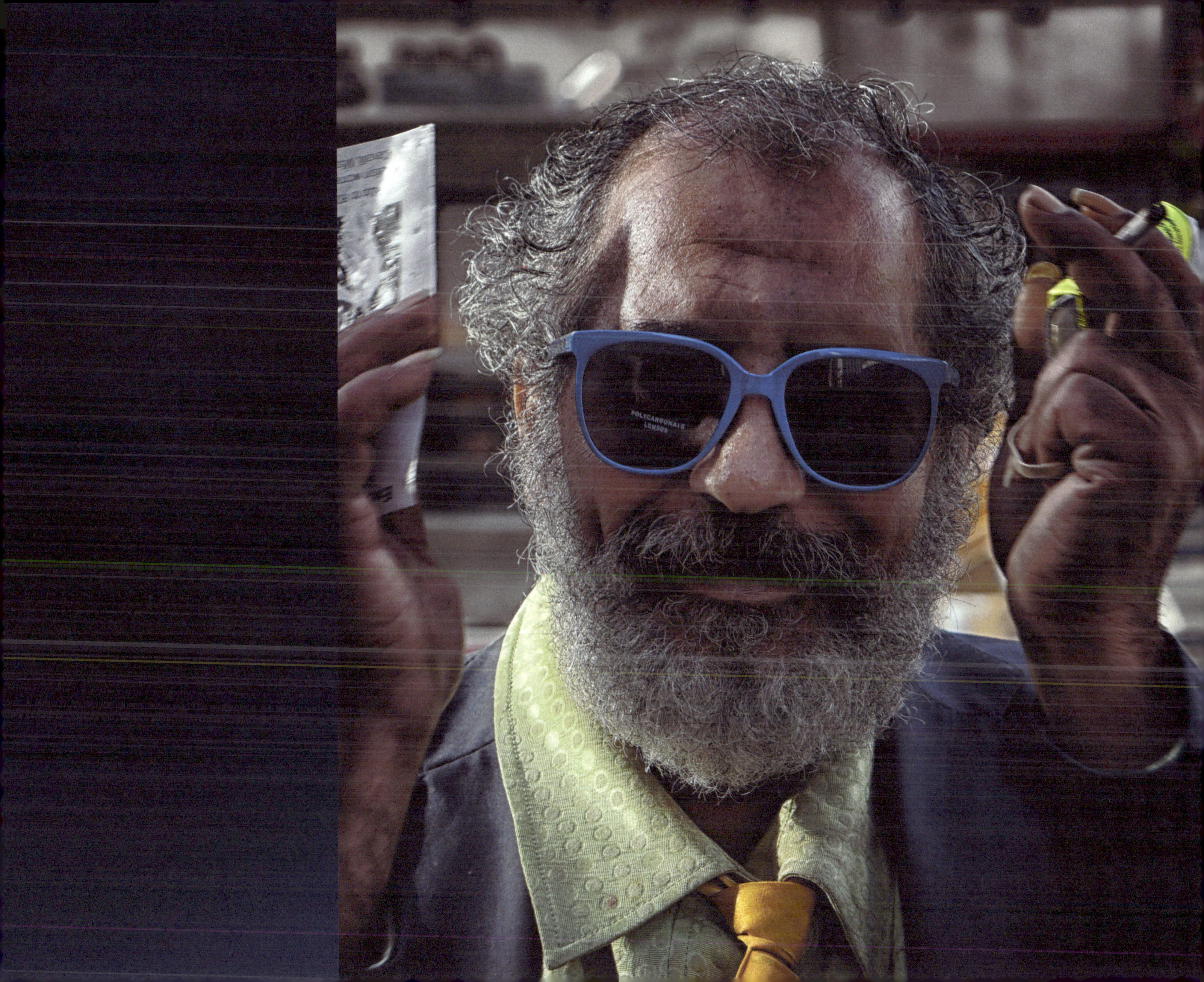

POLYCARBONATE
LENSES

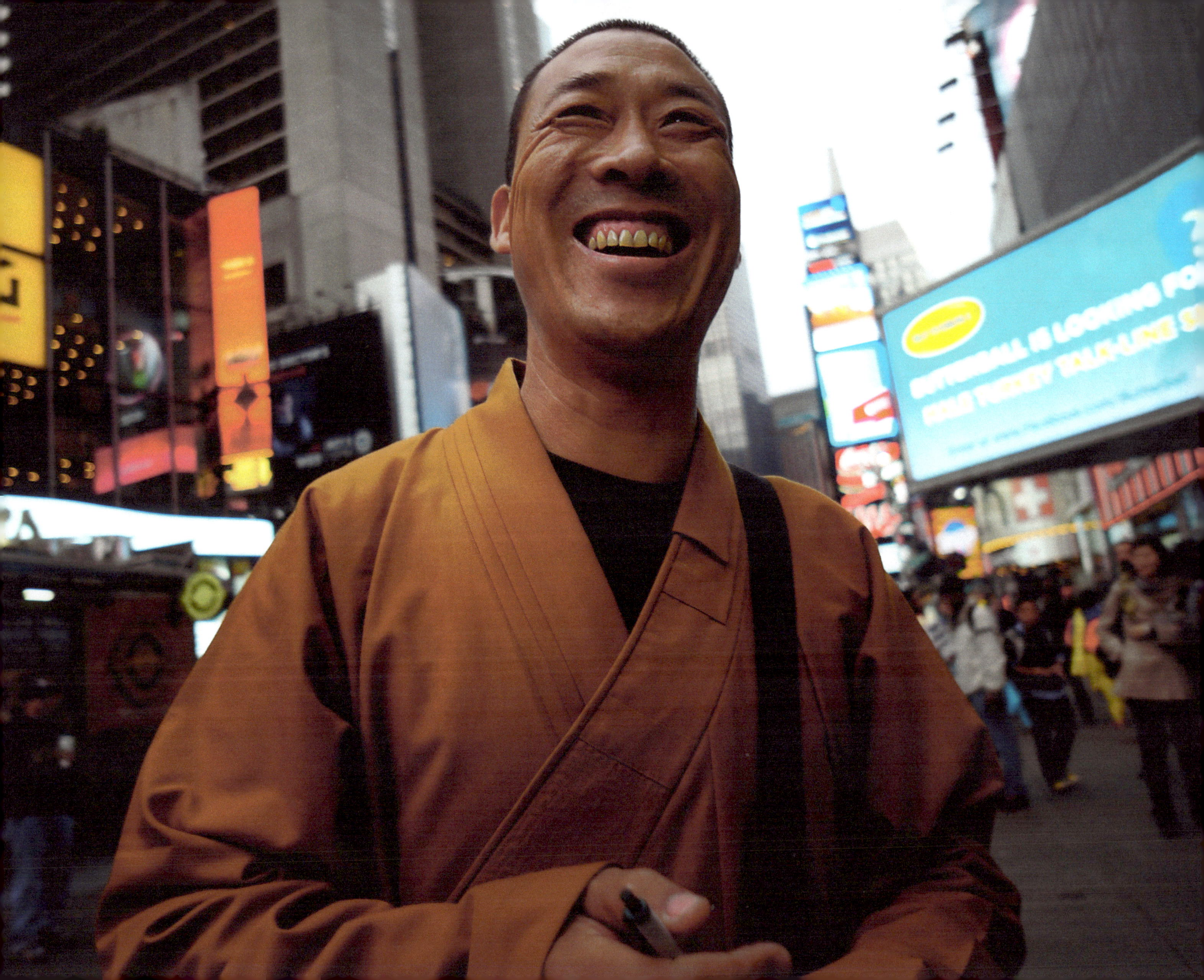

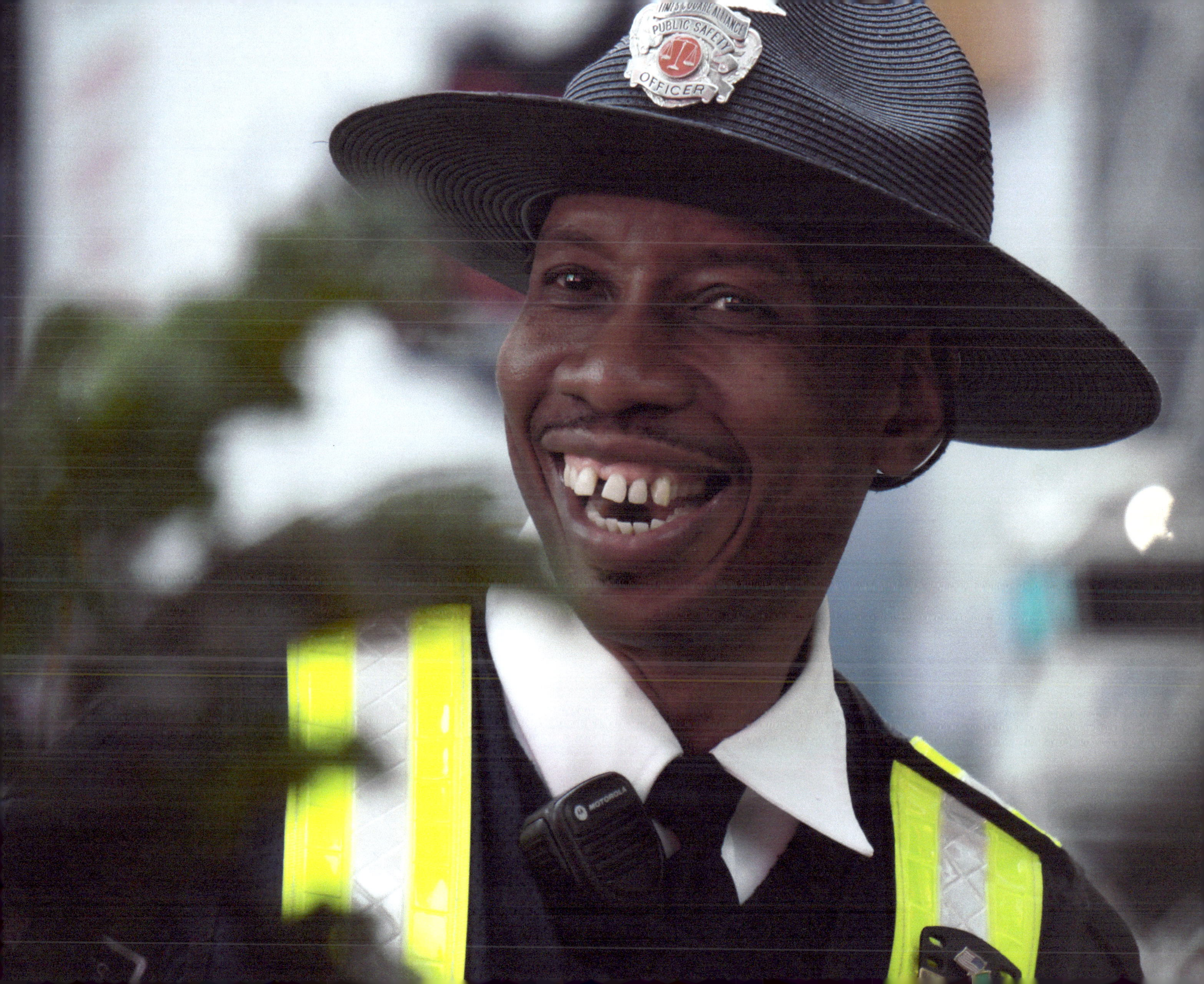

TIMES SQUARE ALLIANCE
PUBLIC SAFETY
OFFICER
MOTOROLA

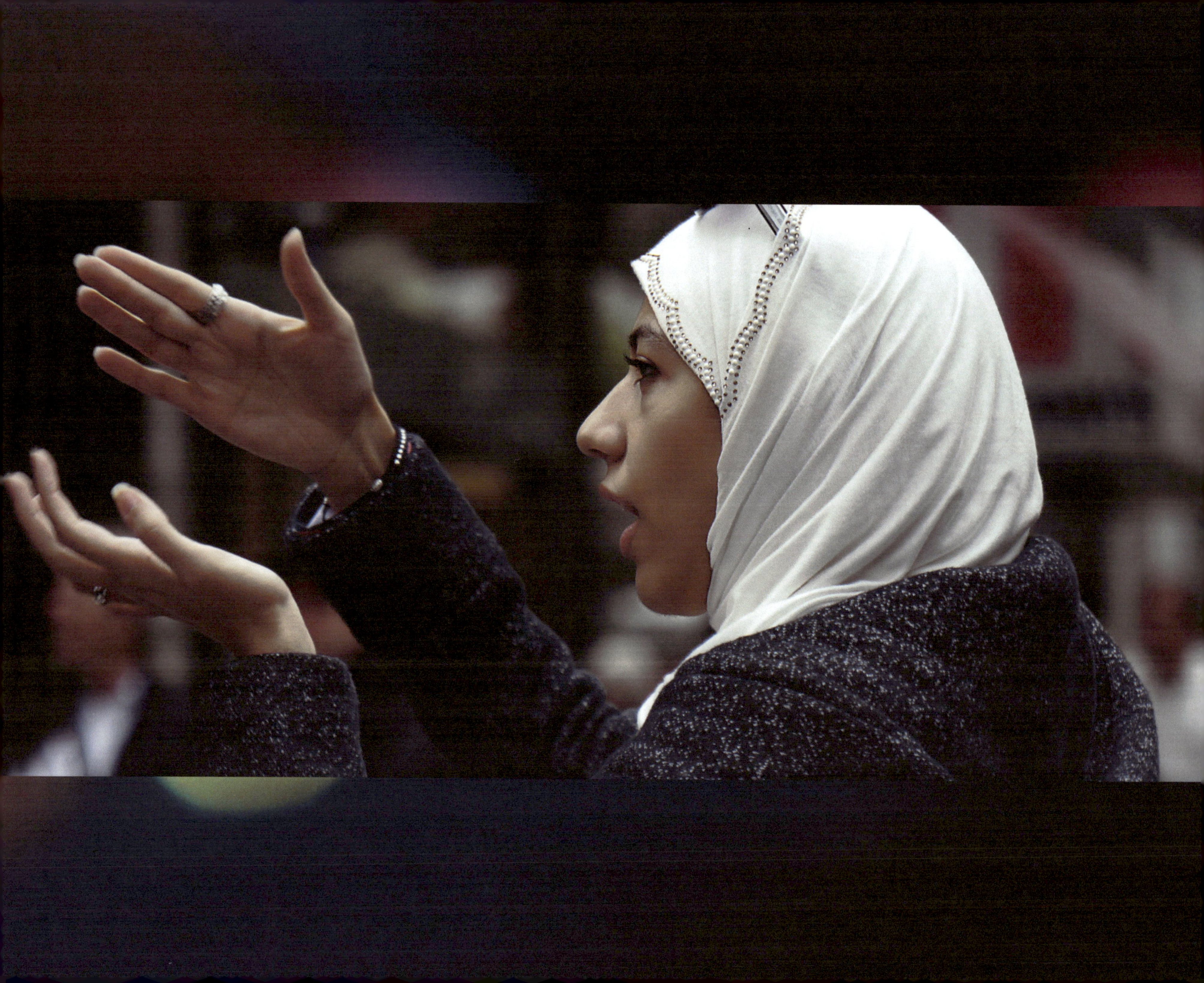

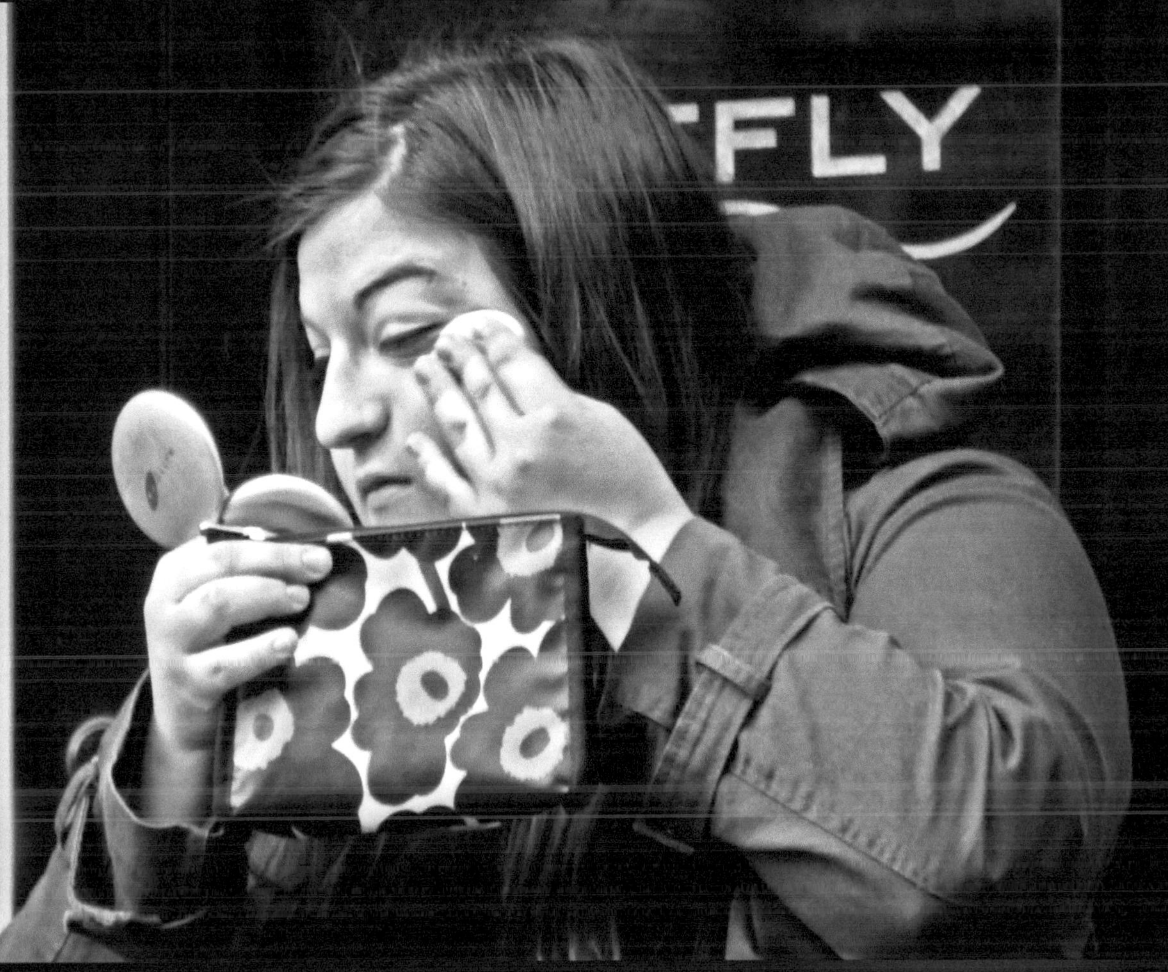
RETAIL
SPACE
FOR RENT
2500 SQ. FT.
TFLY

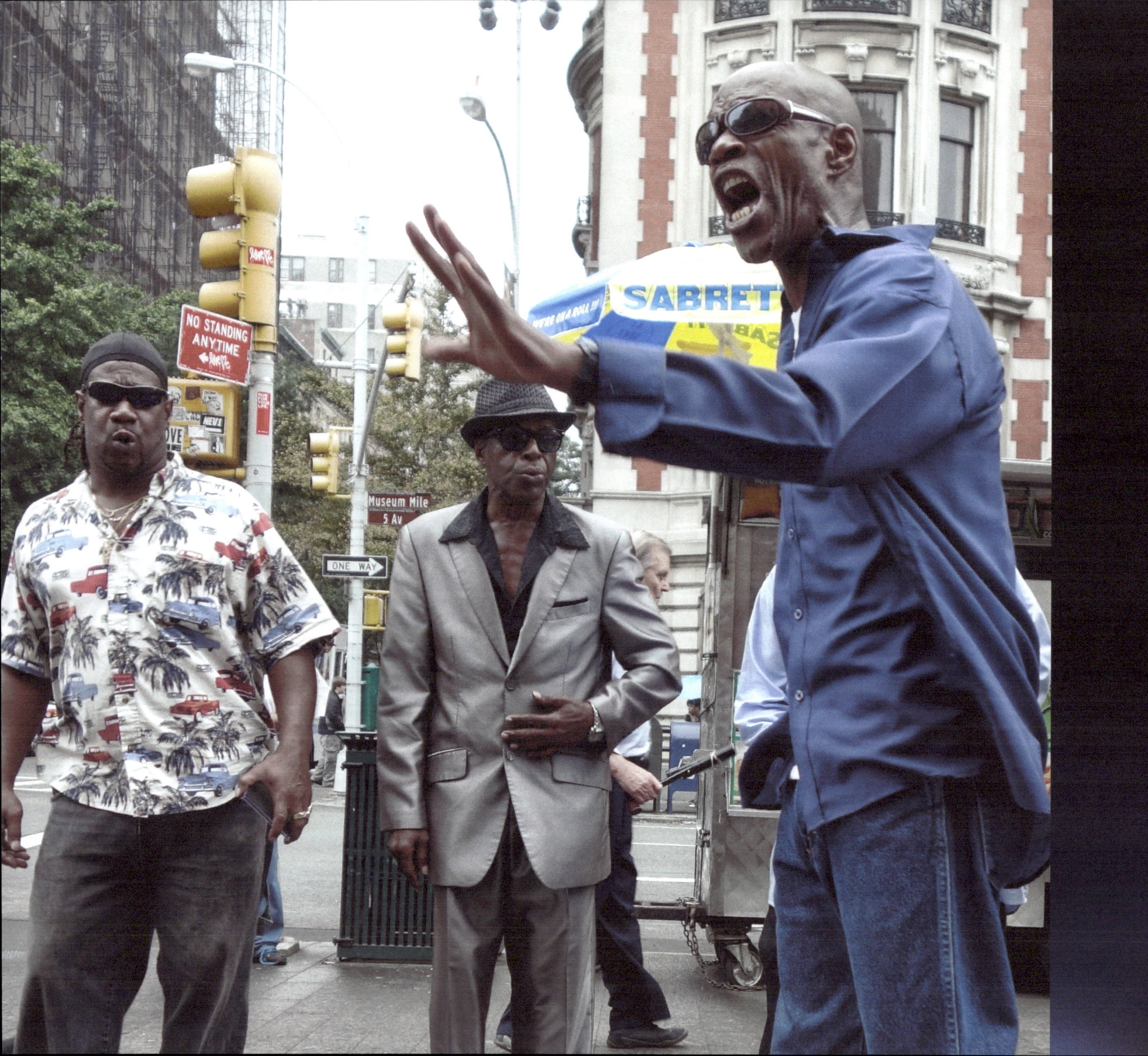

SABRETT
NO STANDING ANYTIME
Museum Mile
5 Av
ONE WAY

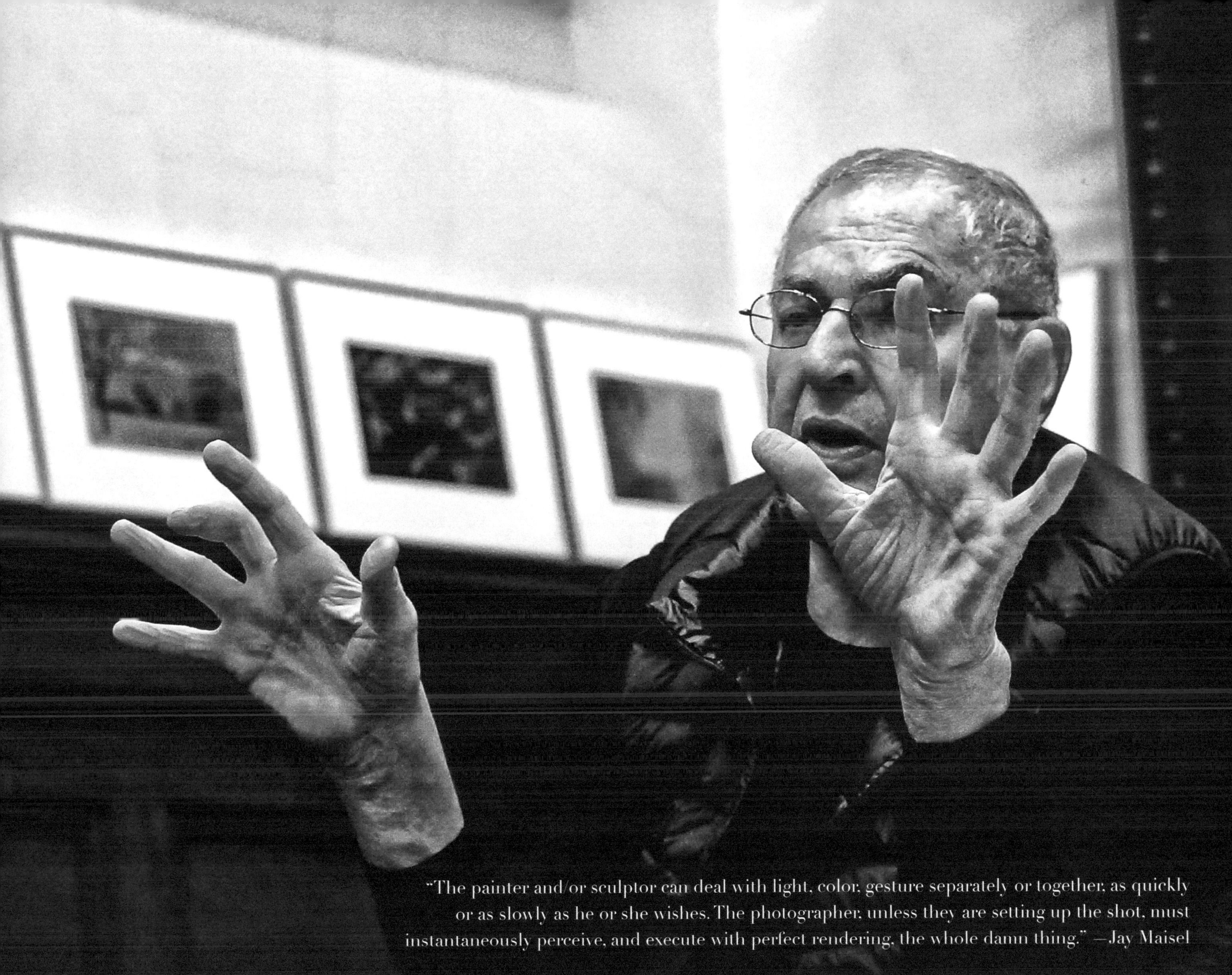
"The painter and/or sculptor can deal with light, color, gesture separately or together, as quickly
or as slowly as he or she wishes. The photographer, unless they are setting up the shot, must
instantaneously perceive, and execute with perfect rendering, the whole damn thing." —Jay Maisel

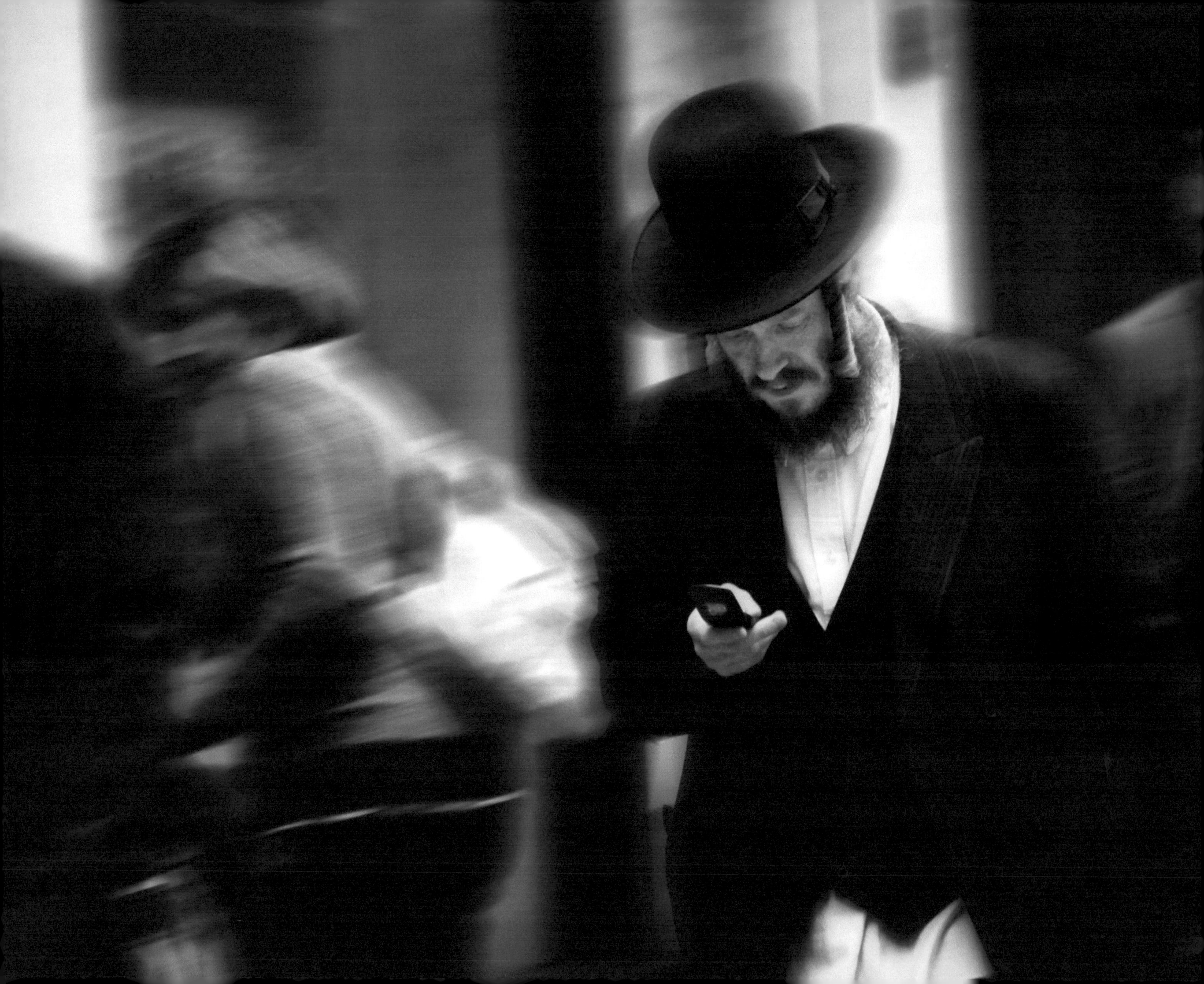

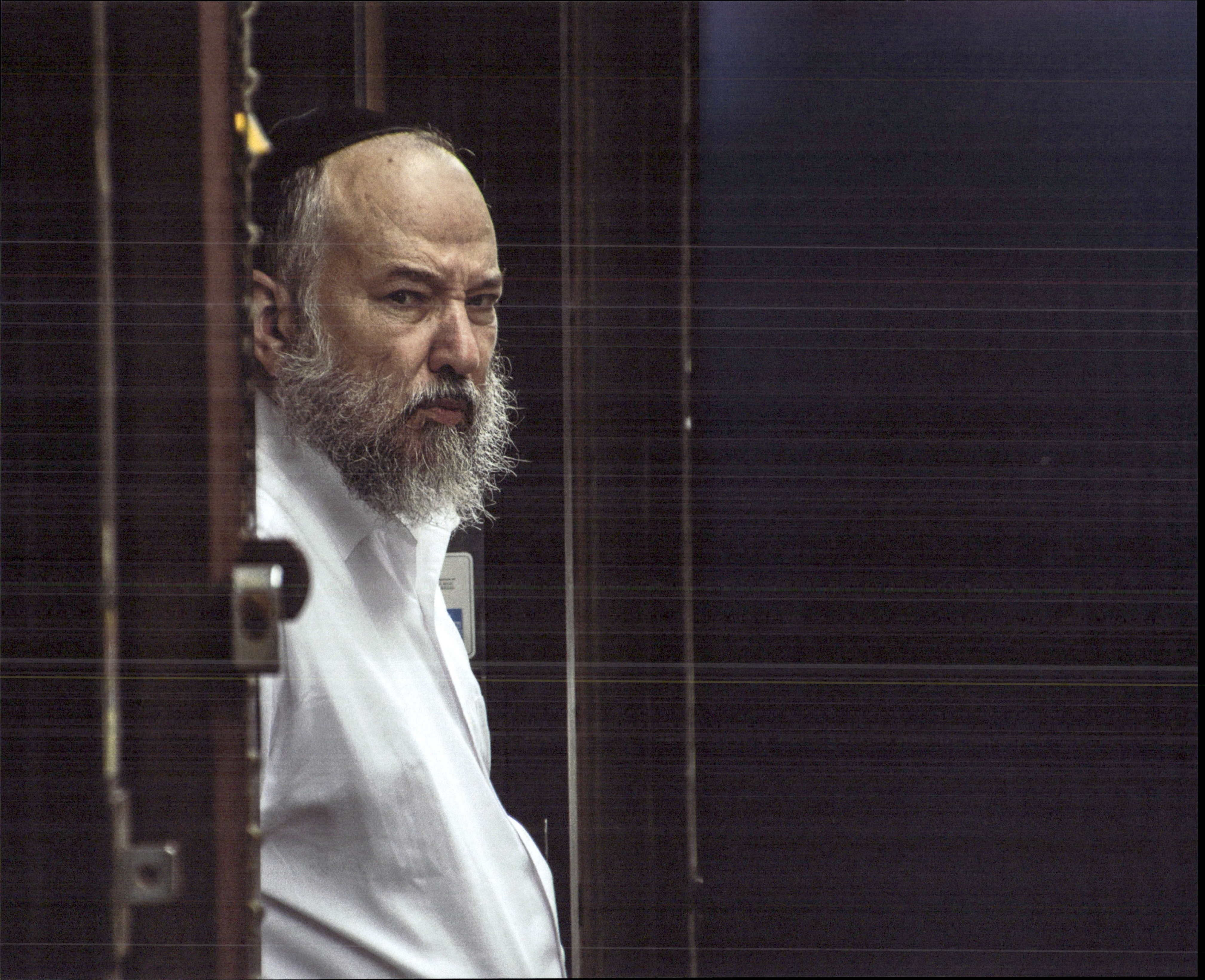

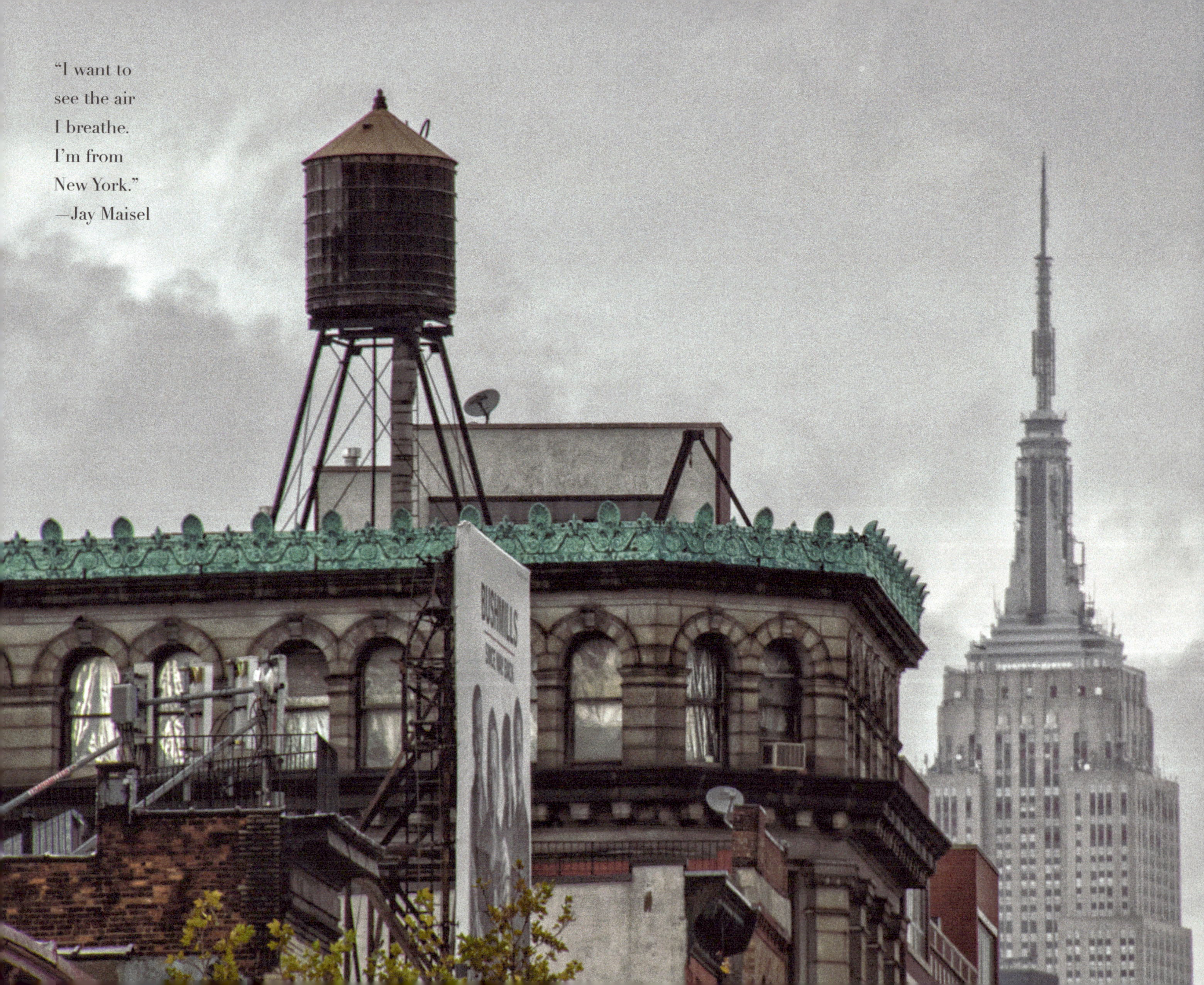

"I want to
see the air
I breathe.
I'm from
New York."
—Jay Maisel

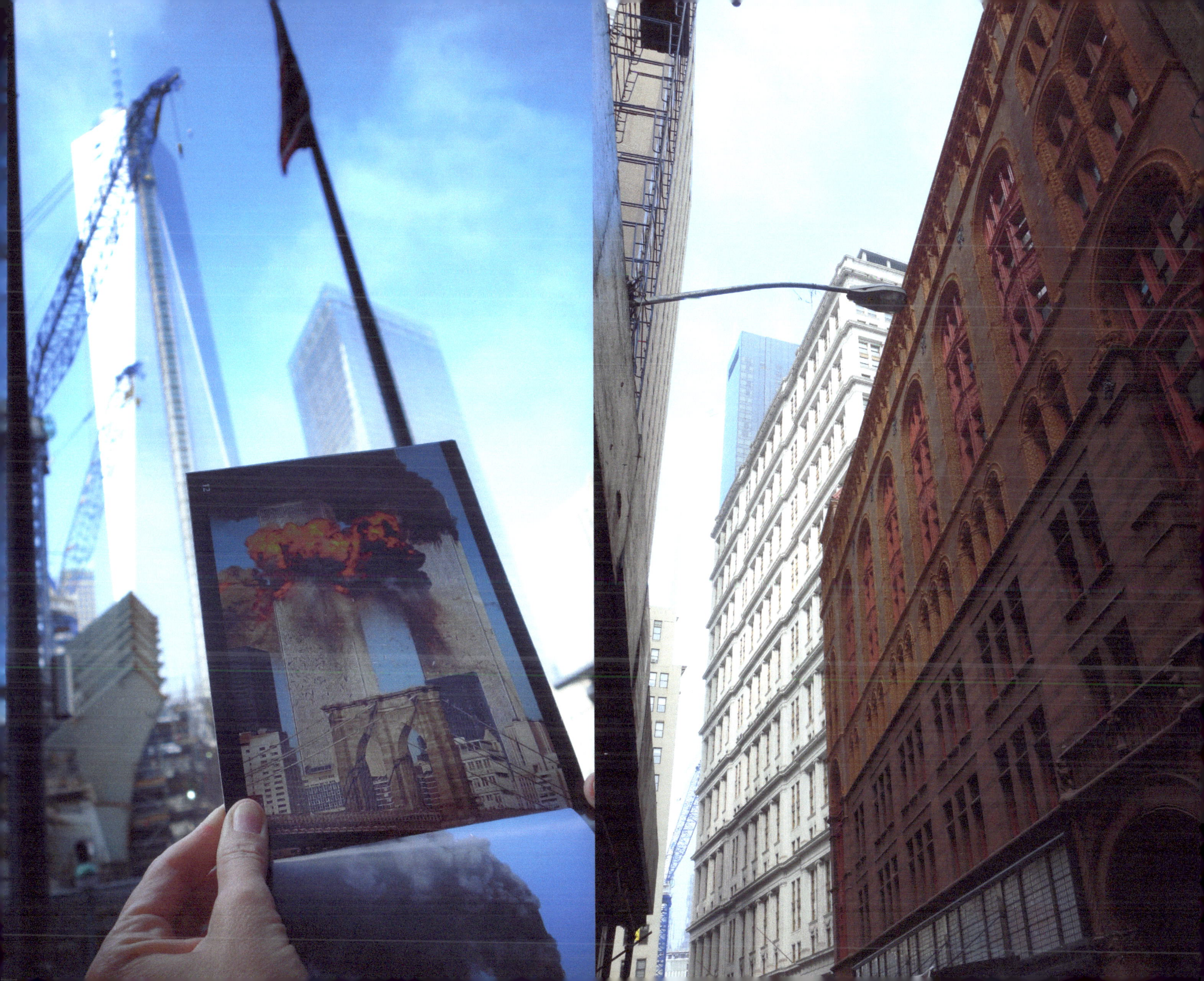

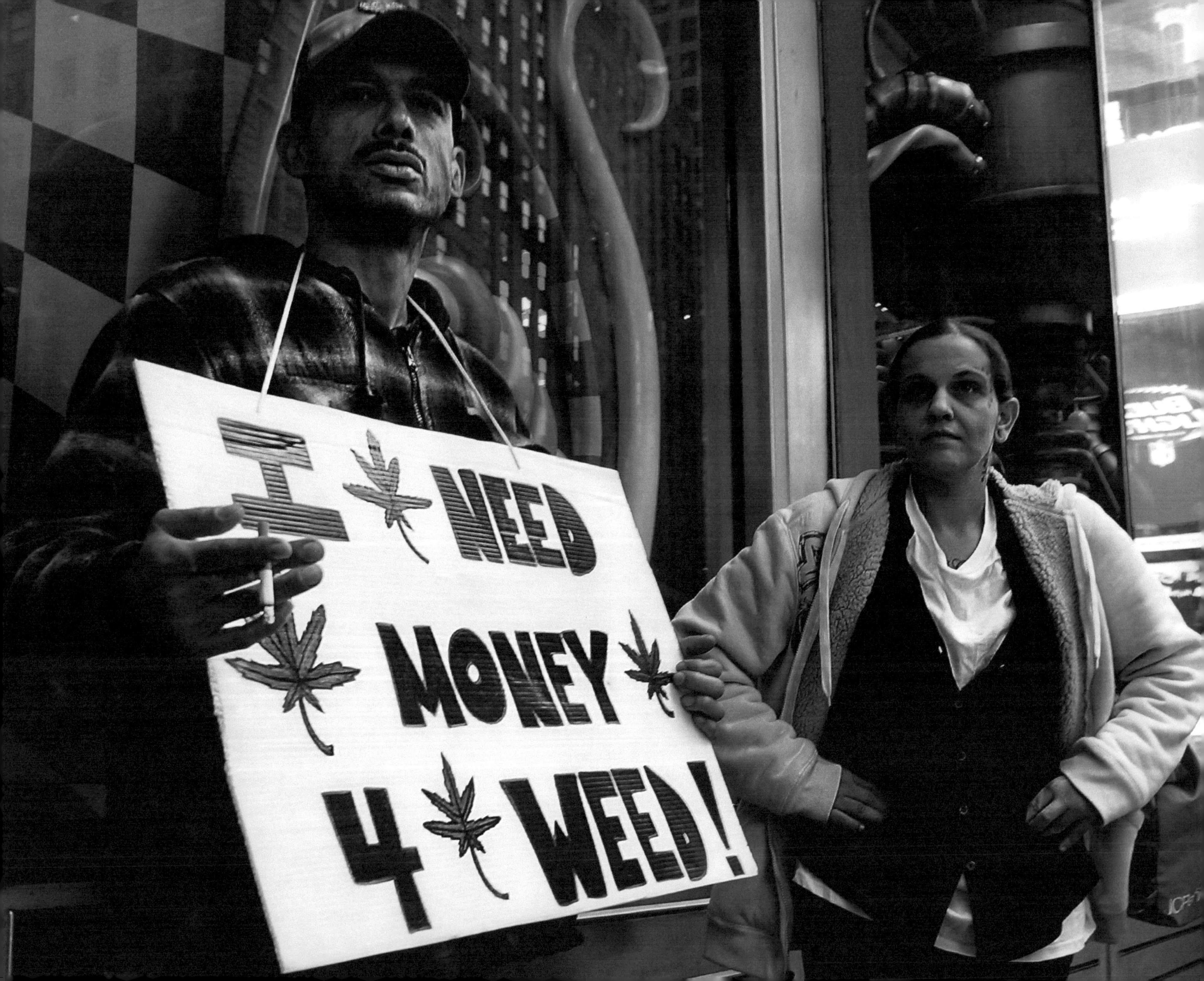

I NEED
MONEY
4 WEED!

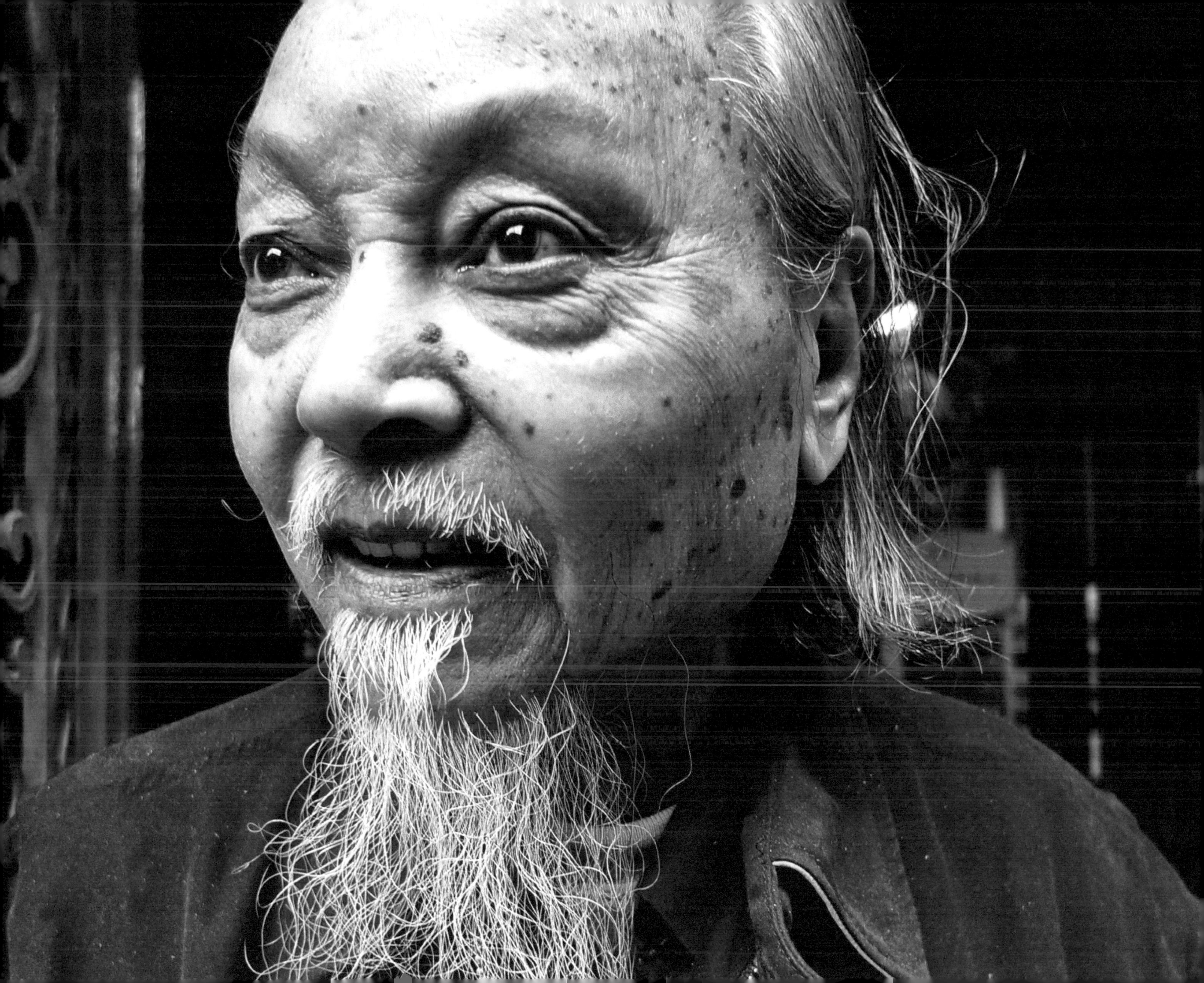

three words of advice on how to become a better photographer

I'M IN A CAB on my way to Penn Station to catch a train to Washington DC. It's a beautiful fall morning in lower Manhattan. I'm exhausted but still inspired from Jay Maisel's week-long photography workshop. His words bounce around my head like the dappled light reflecting off the apartment buildings we pass. I have taken workshops before, but none like this. Jay not only brought me into the world of photographic art, but also challenged me to think about much more.

One theme that came up again and again among the students was overcoming fear. In most cases, students expressed fear of approaching total strangers on the street and asking to take their photographs.

As I watch the streets of New York from the backseat of the cab, I reminisce about the week. I recall how, on the second day of the workshop, I had gone to Grand Central Station and seen a small group of cops standing in a circle and laughing. The light was great, their body language was great. All I had to do was approach and ask the simple favor of a photo. I approached, but by the time my mouth opened, the only courage I had was to ask directions to the subway. By the time I exited on the platform at Bleecker Street, I was angry. Mad at myself for giving into my fears: fear of asking, fear of rejection, fear of failure, fear of the unknown.

As I walked toward the restaurant where Jay's class was meeting for dinner, I took a shortcut into an alley. Two teens were taking photos of each other with their cell phones. They had beautiful faces and were dressed with a style all their own—lots of bling. I desperately wanted to shoot photographs of them. Still feeling silly and ashamed about the cops in the train station, I took a deep breath and walked up. My small camera was still stowed in my shoulder bag. I explained who I was and what I needed. I brought out a few of my business cards to offer some credibility. Within a few minutes, I was in the middle of my own photo shoot in the alley. Minutes later, I was off down the street, having just made two new friends.

A block later, a young model walked past me with the longest legs I had ever seen, going all the way up to a short skirt. I wanted to photograph her legs, but I couldn't just walk up and say, "Hey, I love your legs, how about if I photograph them?" Instead, I walked past, pausing to ask her if I was going in the right direction to Spring Street. She was willing to help. Then, in a by-the-way comment, I remarked, "You have the coolest shoes. Would you mind if I took a photograph of them?"

"You want to photograph my shoes? Uh, Sure." In a second, I was gone. Another friend made. *(continued…)*

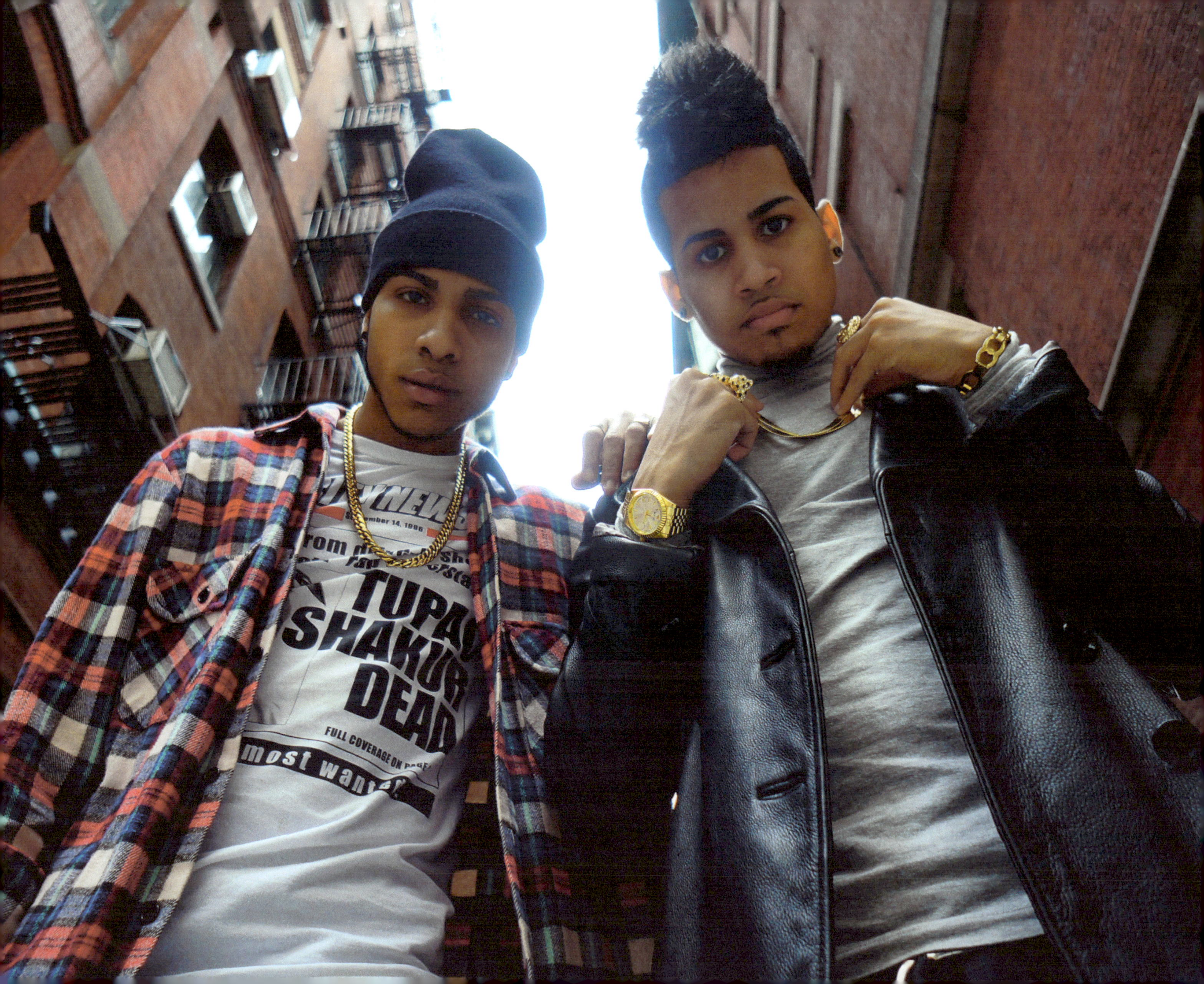
TUPAC
SHAKUR
DEAD
FULL COVERAGE ON PAGE
most wanted

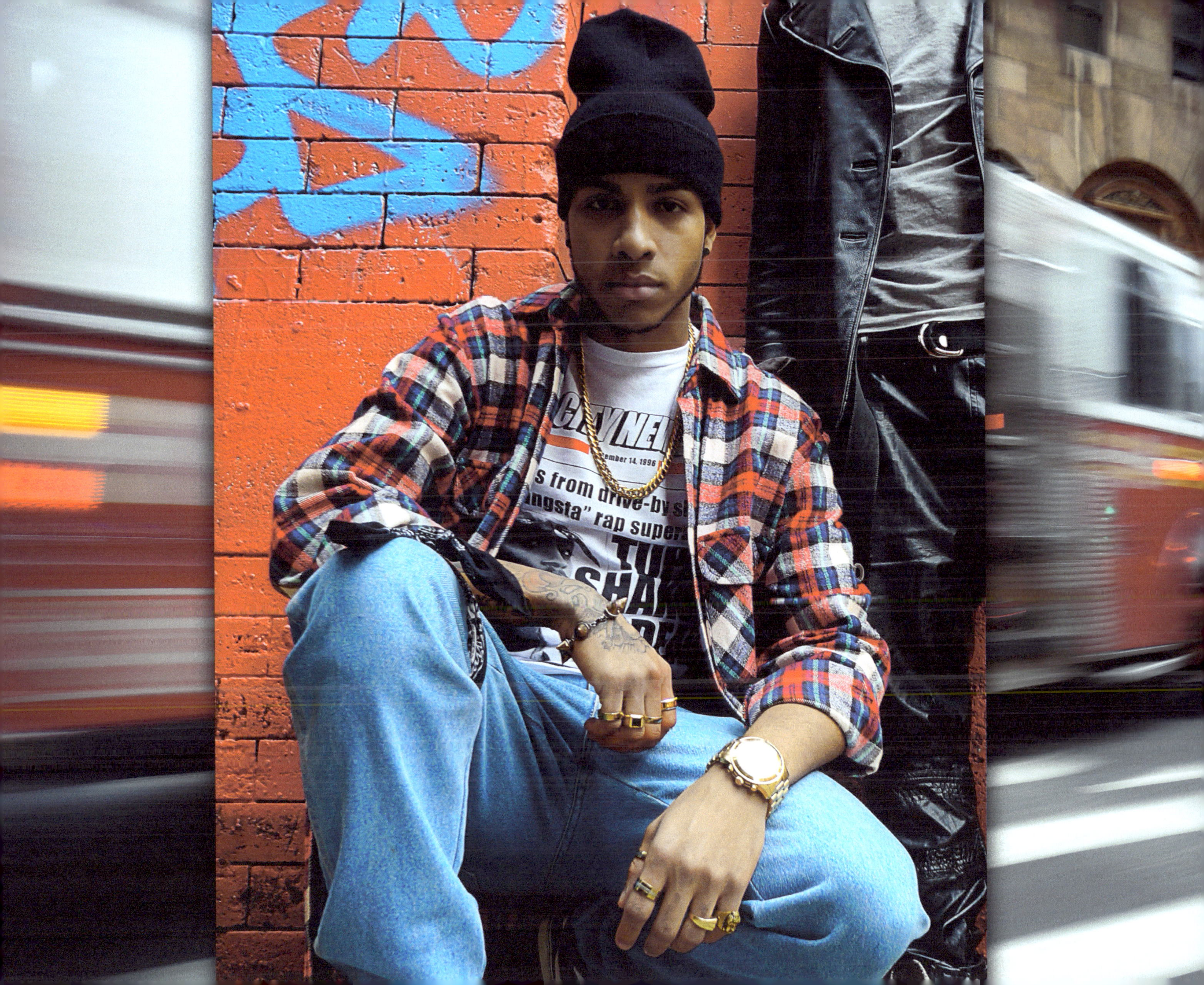
s from drive-by sh
ngsta" rap supers
ember 14, 1996

A FEW BLOCKS LATER, I ran into a photographer from the workshop, also looking for our restaurant. While my energy was pumped and brimming, he was sad and sinking.

"How did your afternoon go with shooting?"

"Not well. Not well at all," he said. "I just can't get it together enough to walk up to total strangers and ask to take their photos."

I put my arm around him, now confident that I had (in the last few blocks) mastered my universe, and overcome the one thing that holds us back from achieving the things we all yearn to conquer: fear.

"Buddy-boy," I said, smiling. "We are going to blow that fear right out the window, right now!"

He looked at me with an expression that reminded me I was showing off and that whatever I did would not get him out of his foxhole.

I continued on as if I was Captain Courageous, leading my mate into battle. "You pick out anyone on this street and I am going to show you how it's done."

"Ok, how about those guys?" He pointed to a couple of black dudes leaning on a mailbox, talking. My stomach tightened, but I had committed myself, so I stepped to the edge of the diving board, ready to leap.

A few minutes later, I had made two new friends and taken two new portraits.

My classmate was not impressed. As we walked toward the restaurant, he made a remark about how it really helped having been born with a bubbly personality.

Idiot.

AFTER DINNER, as we regrouped around Jay's conference table for another late-night discussion, I raised my hand to tell my story. I was pumped up as if I had finally discovered what was too simple to be a Eureka moment.

I talked about my day: the cops, the others I had approached but dodged, and how I finally got so upset at myself that I refused to give into my fears any longer. I continued on about how I met the kids in the ally, then the girl with the long legs, then…

I talked about fear as the demon that holds us all back from accomplishing the things we really want: from asking our boss for a raise or asking the beauty to the prom. My rant continued as I told the story of my son Quincy, nineteen years ago, as a baby, about to take his first step.

"So my baby boy stood there on the carpet, wanting so much to walk, leaning forward. Finally, his leg extended, he leaned into it, fully committed.

(continued…)

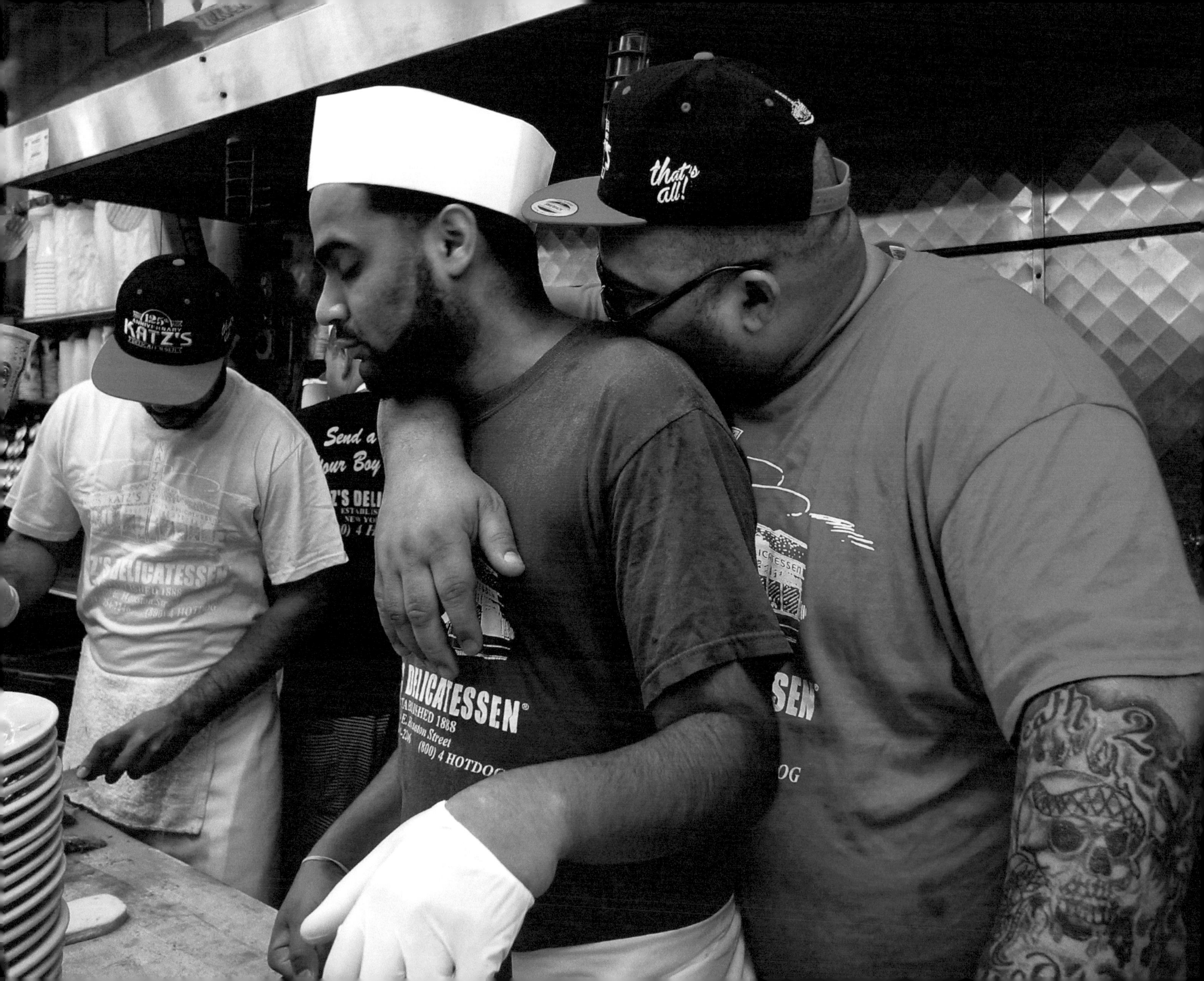

that's all!
125th ANNIVERSARY
KATZ'S
DELICATESSEN
Send a
Your Boy
KATZ'S DELI
ESTABLISHED 1888
NEW YO
(800) 4 H
KATZ'S DELICATESSEN
ESTABLISHED 1888
Houston St
(800) 4 HOTDOG
DELICATESSEN®
ESTABLISHED 1888
E. Houston Street
(800) 4 HOTDOG

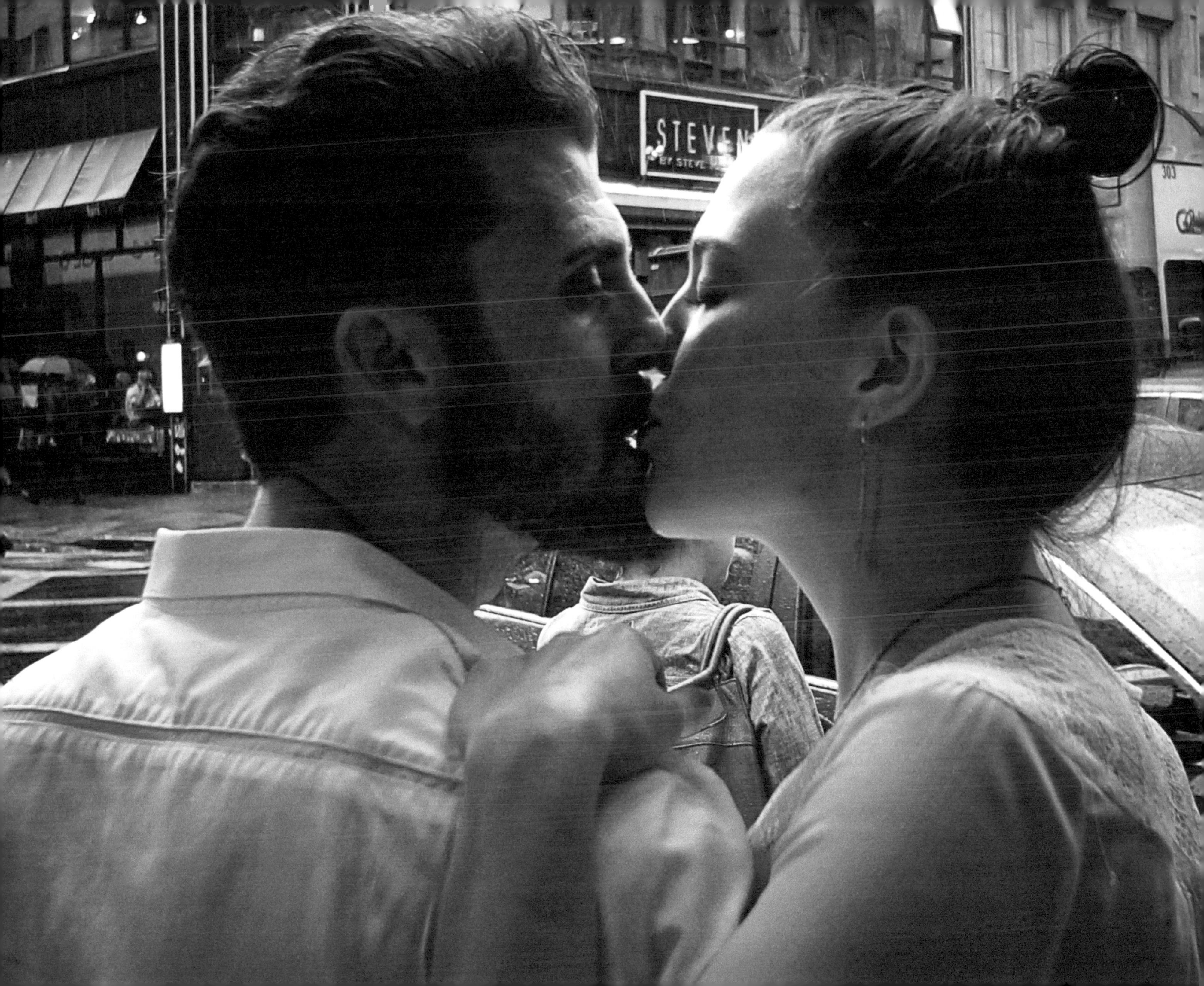

STEVEN
BY STEVE
303

I watched this in awe and realized that a step forward, literally and figuratively, was just an interrupted fall. We all have to risk falling if we are going to make headway in this life."

I wasn't finished. By now, everyone was looking at me as though I were asking them to walk across burning coals. "Okay, tomorrow, I promise you that I am going to walk up, without hesitation, to everyone I want to photograph, especially cops! The next day, I'm going to up the ante and find some hookers on the street to do portraits of! (Now the laugher started.) And the day after that I'm going to up it again and do portraits of mob bosses! I am done with this fear thing!"

I smacked my palm down on the conference table to emphasize my point.

I half expected the entire group to leap to their feet, cheering me on, recognizing that I was the one to lead them to glory.

No one said a word.

Jay looked at me and quietly offered, "I've never heard it expressed quite like that."

THE NEXT MORNING, I was up at dawn and walking the streets of China Town. I made more friends. My new friends delivered fresh fish. Others were opening their shops. Still others rode on the backs of garbage trucks.

Along the way, I came up with a new way to play the game of Tag. While walking down the sidewalk, I spotted a crossing guard I wanted to photograph. Instead of stopping, I smiled as I walked past and said simply, "Good morning." She smiled back. She didn't know it but she had just been tagged. I kept walking and went about photographing some merchants. Then, I passed the crossing guard again. "What a day!" I exclaimed. She agreed and was thus tagged a second time. My tags were building a relationship. After searching for more photos in the surrounding neighborhood, I circled back one last time.

By now we knew each other– well, sort of. "Have you worked in this neighborhood a long time?" I asked.

"Oh yes," she replied with warm smile. "It's getting close to twelve years."

"You must know the names of every family on the block! I bet you have seen a lot of their kids grow up through the years."

"I know their names. I know all their stories."

She was smiling, so proud of what she does every morning, so proud of her role in the neighborhood.

"Where are you from?" she asked.

(continued…)

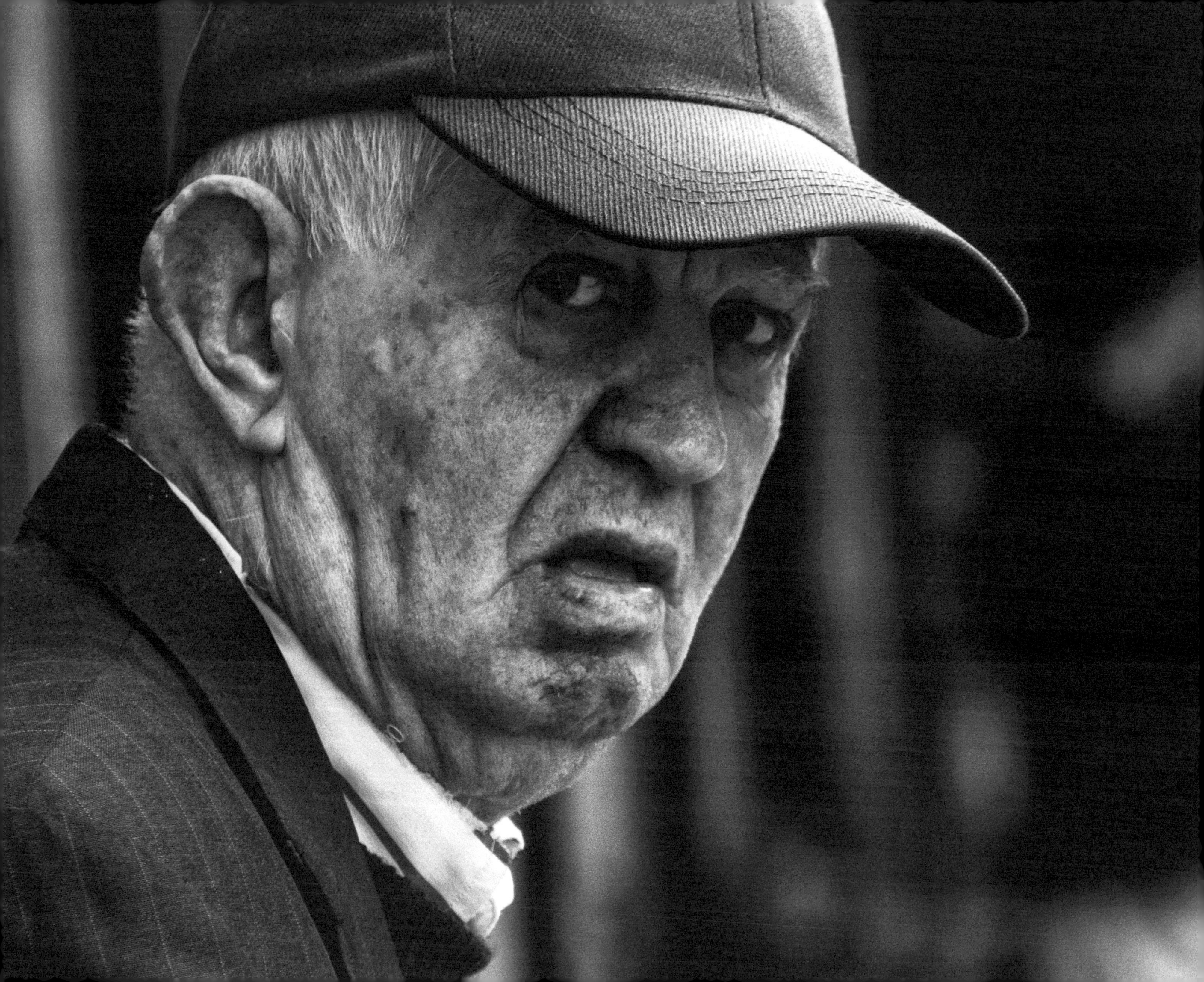

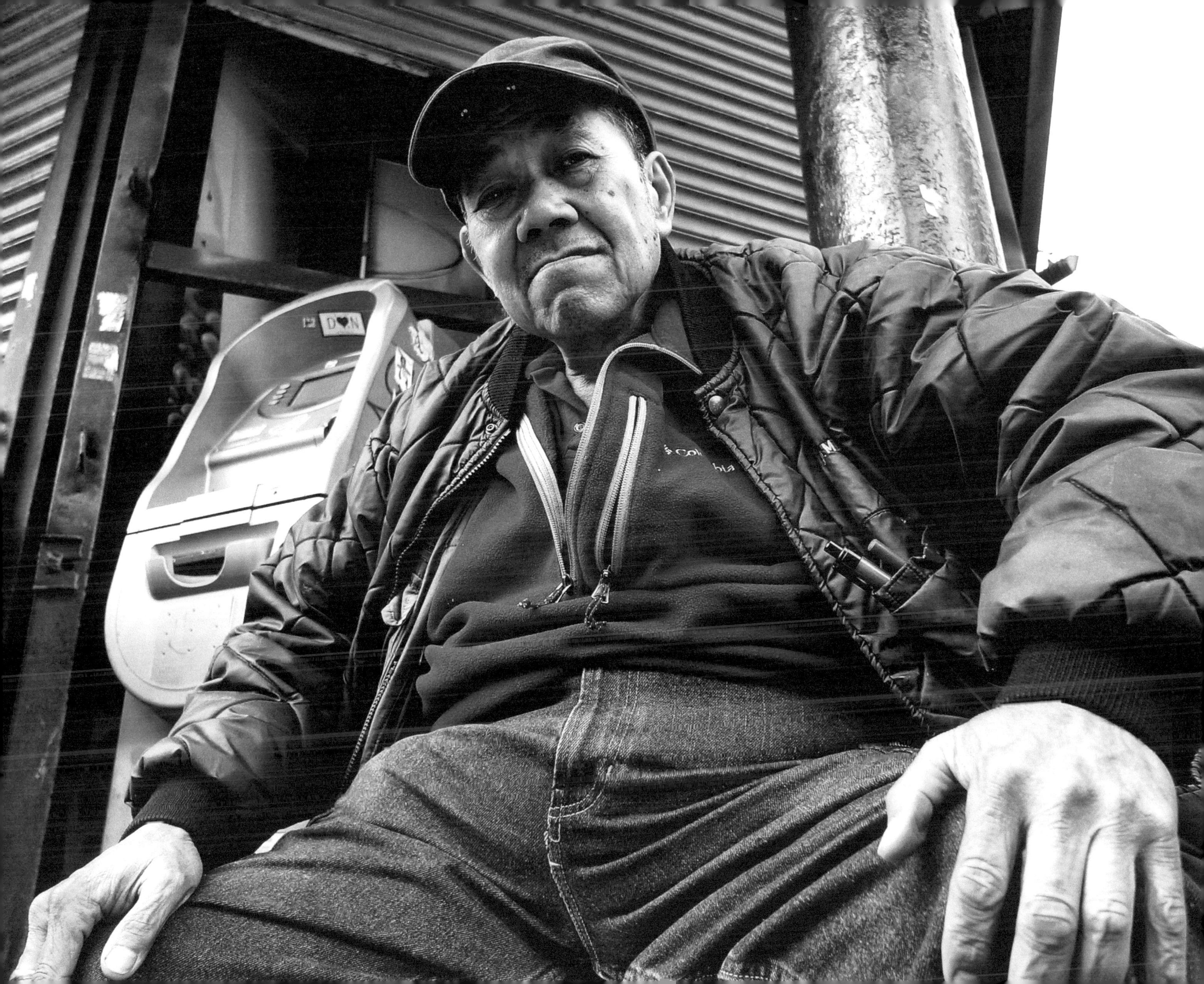
D♥N

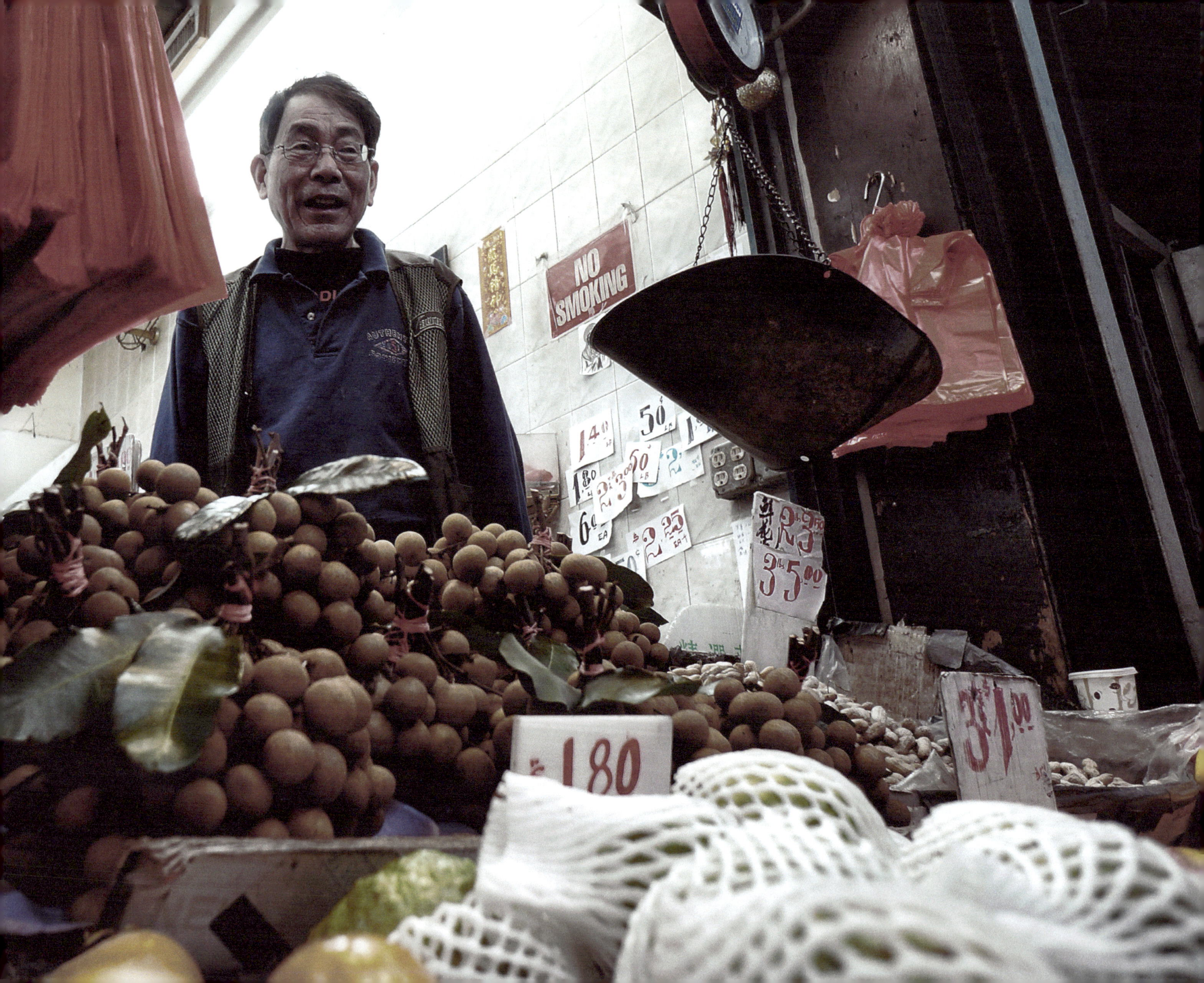

NO
SMOKING
1.80

"West Coast. I'm a photographer here to take photographs of interesting people in New York." Then I brought out a few of my cards, all with different portraits on them.

"You took all these?!" she questioned, still smiling.

Now I was the proud one.

"Absolutely. By the way, would you mind if I took your photograph?"

Bingo.

Her name was Lydia.

I will never forget that early morning. Though her photograph did not make the final edit and get her the page she deserves, the memory of our encounter will last just as long. As two strangers on the corner in China Town, we offered each other a small peek into our worlds, putting aside our fear and apprehension, to have a brief connection in the warming morning sun.

Thank you, Lydia.

That was a turning point for me. For the rest of the week, I made friends wherever I went. Most were happy to let me photograph them.

(continued...)

Except for the boxer. He was jogging down the side of the street, snorting like an older, black Rocky, in traditional sweats, boxing gloves jabbing at some invisible opponent. I dashed up to him, snapping away. He covered his face as if being assaulted in the ring.

'"What the hell you do'n?! Why you taken my picha?!"

"Because you have such a great face!" I offered.

"What?!" Clearly offended. "You some kind of fag?!"

I thought he was going to take a swing at me. I slowed down, hoping he would keep going. I was disappointed. I had been on such a roll. But how do you "tag" a boxer?

WITH THE WORKSHOP BEHIND ME NOW, my cab moves through the light Saturday morning traffic. For the first time, I am glad the driver is speeding. I am afraid I am going to miss my train. Then, as if in slow motion, my head turns and I see what appears to be something out of a movie. A beautiful woman, long brown hair, graceful as tall grass blowing in the wind, is doing a cartwheel in the middle of a distant side street. She is a ballerina dressed in a flesh-colored leotard. As my taxi accelerates, my head continues to turn to drink in this amazing sight that can only happen in New York. She disappears and I turn my attention back to the road ahead, again focused on making it to the train in time.

(continued...)

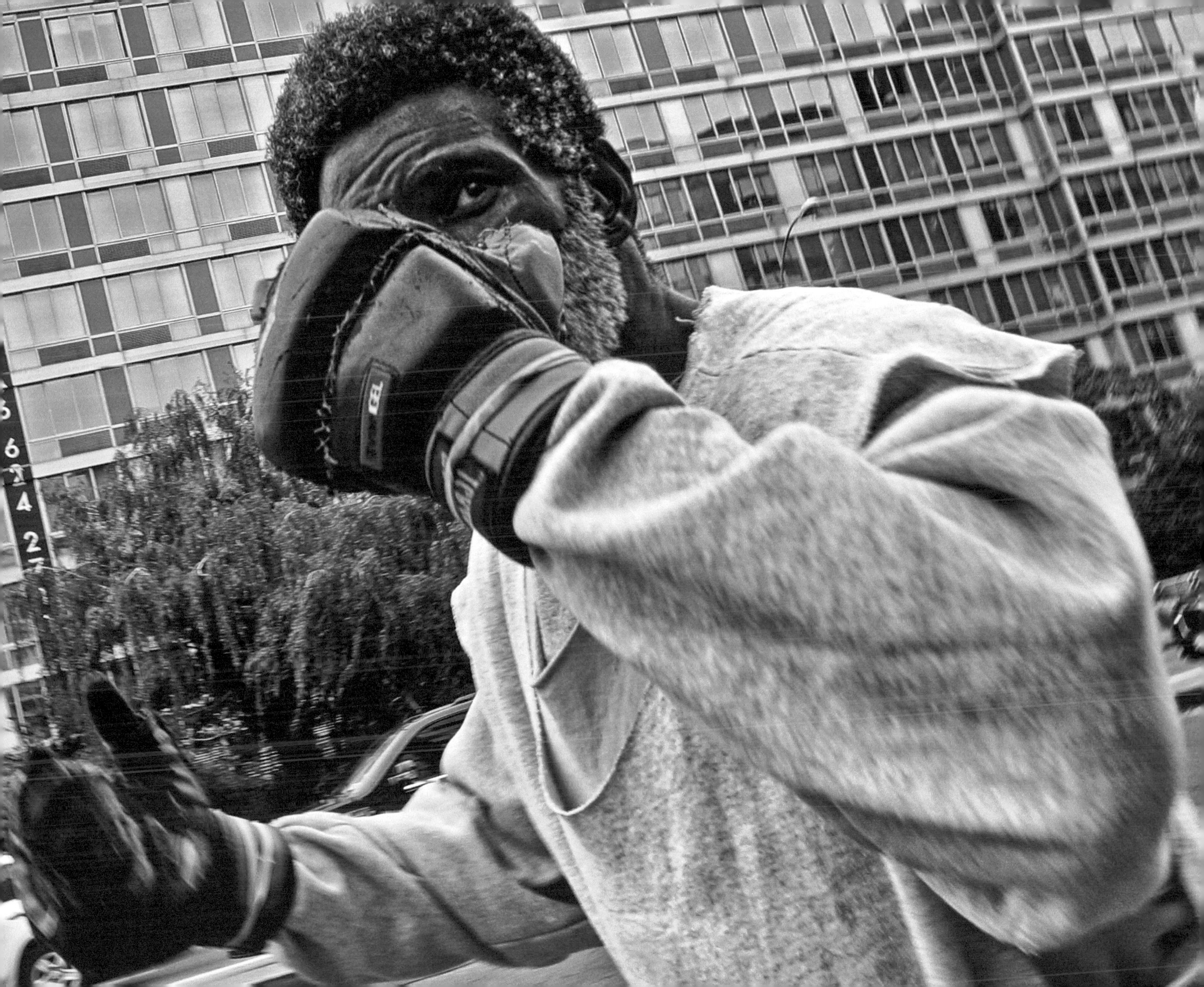

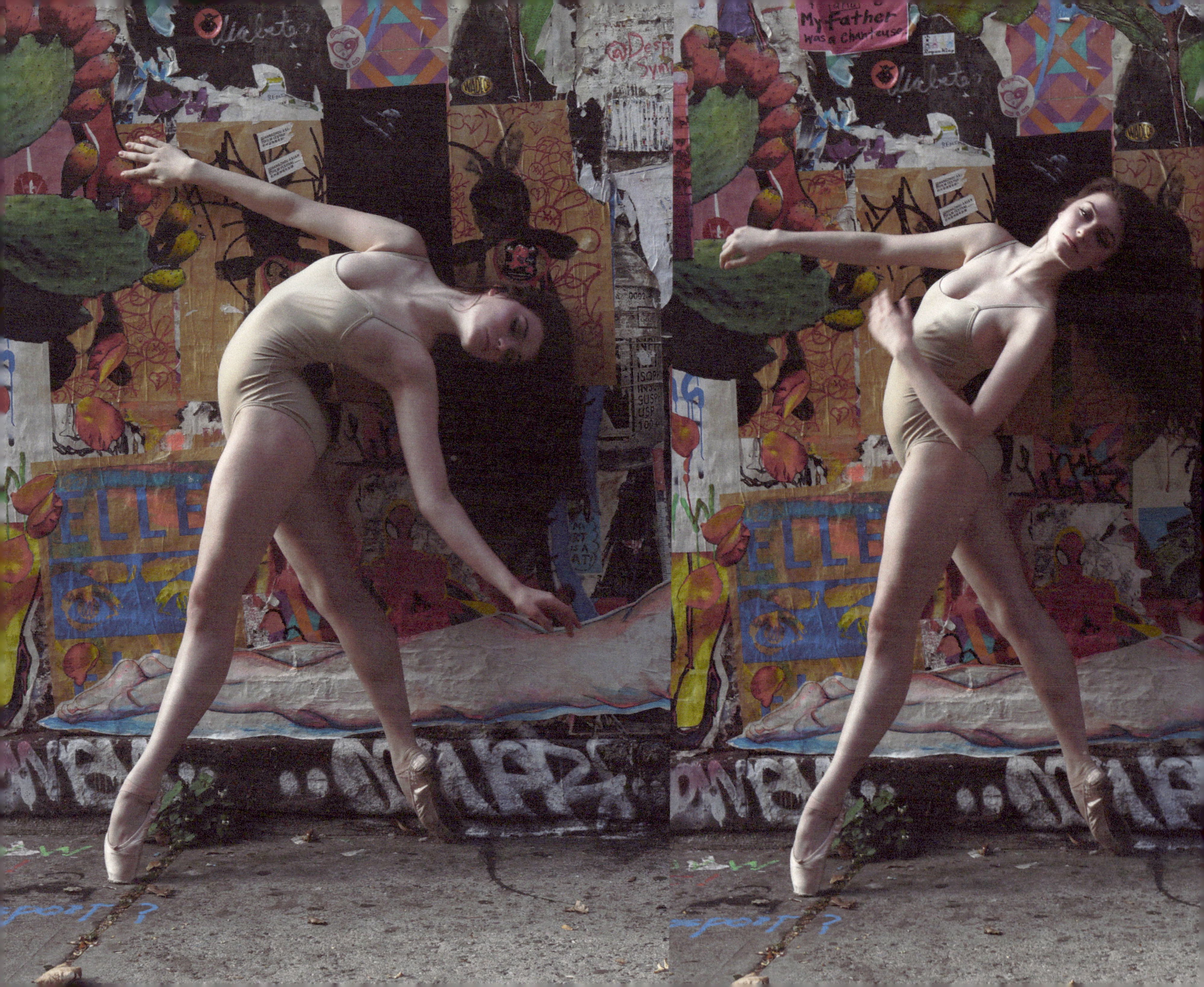

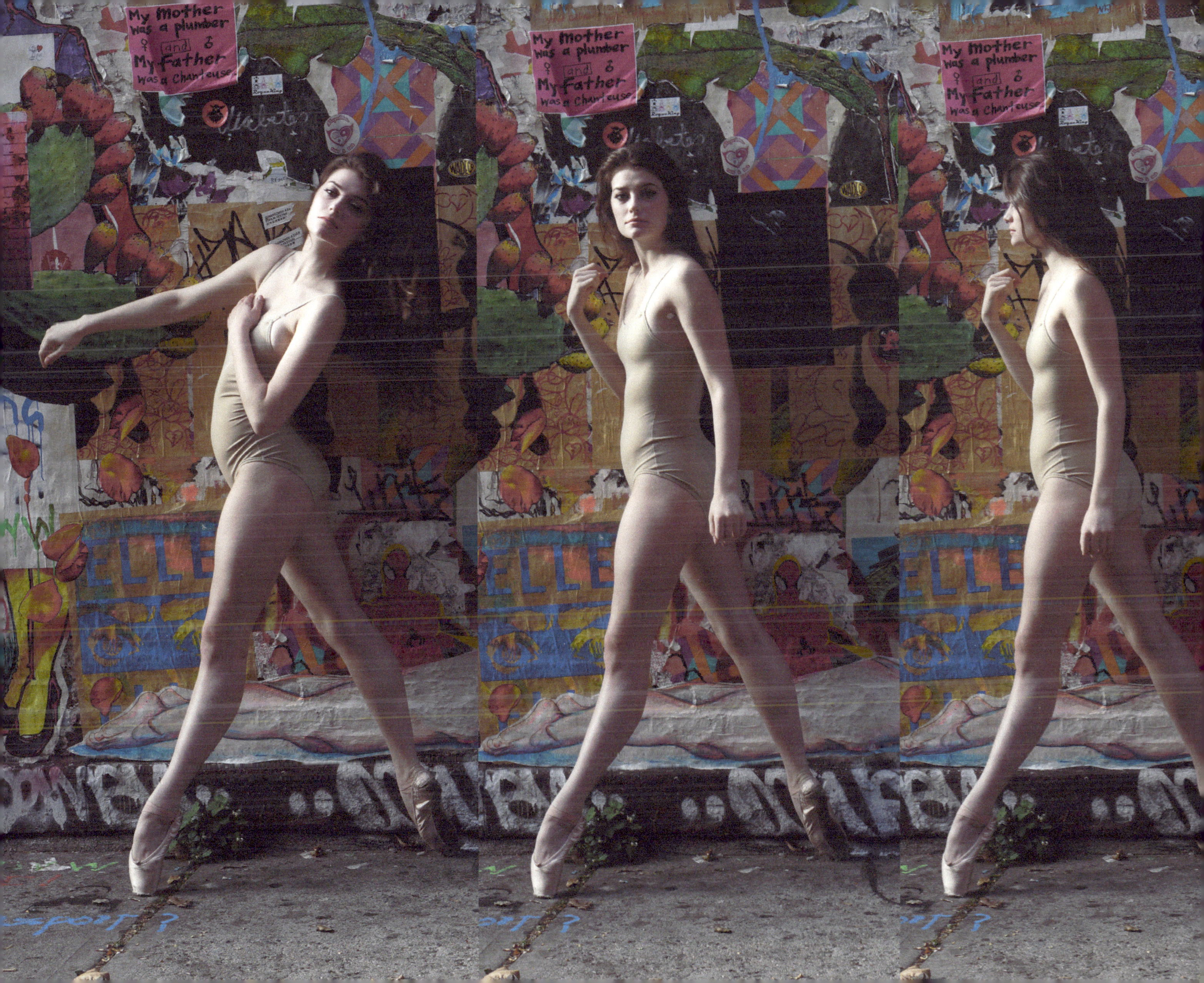

My Mother
was a plumber
♀ [and] ♂
My Father
was a Chanteuse

Maisel's mantra about gesture starts to play in my head. "Gesture will always reveal narrative, which light and color alone find it difficult to do. Gesture can tell a story."

The ballerina in the street seems to embody nearly everything Jay has been trying to tell me during the past five days. Although she is now blocks away, the light on her face, the color, and her amazing grace and gesture stays with me. Gesture. She has it all. But I am late and my old habits are already taking hold. Somehow getting to the train on time takes precedence over getting out of the cab and trying to capture the essence of everything I came to learn in Jay's workshop.

Fear is the mother of procrastination.

I finally wake up.

"Pull over! Now!"

"But I thought we were go'n to Penn Station!"

"Pull over!"

"You da boss."

With my suitcase in tow and juggling two other carry-ons, I run down the sidewalk. I am not sure where I'm headed. All I really know is that I have to try to find her. I am a photographer. I take pictures. As Jay says, "Carrying a camera is a way of life, it's an obligation." I no longer get on trains just because they are in the station.

The Princess of Gesture is there, teasing me, testing me, in the streets of Manhattan.

ALMOST OUT OF BREATH, I round a corner, about to give up and hail another cab. At least I've tried. Then, right in front of me, mere steps away, is the ballerina. I don't have time to make friends or ask her name. I don't have time to ask her to pose. I am not sure what to do. Then, suddenly, as if channeled by Jay himself, she arches her back, ever so slowly, in front of a wall of colorful, posted signs. With my small camera in hand, I press the shutter button. Just hold it down and pray. She looks up at me, almost startled. I smile, then mouth the words, "THANK YOU." I jump into a cab and am gone.

Jay Maisel's voice comes into my head again.

"The three words of advice on how to become a better photographer are: MOVE YOUR ASS! "

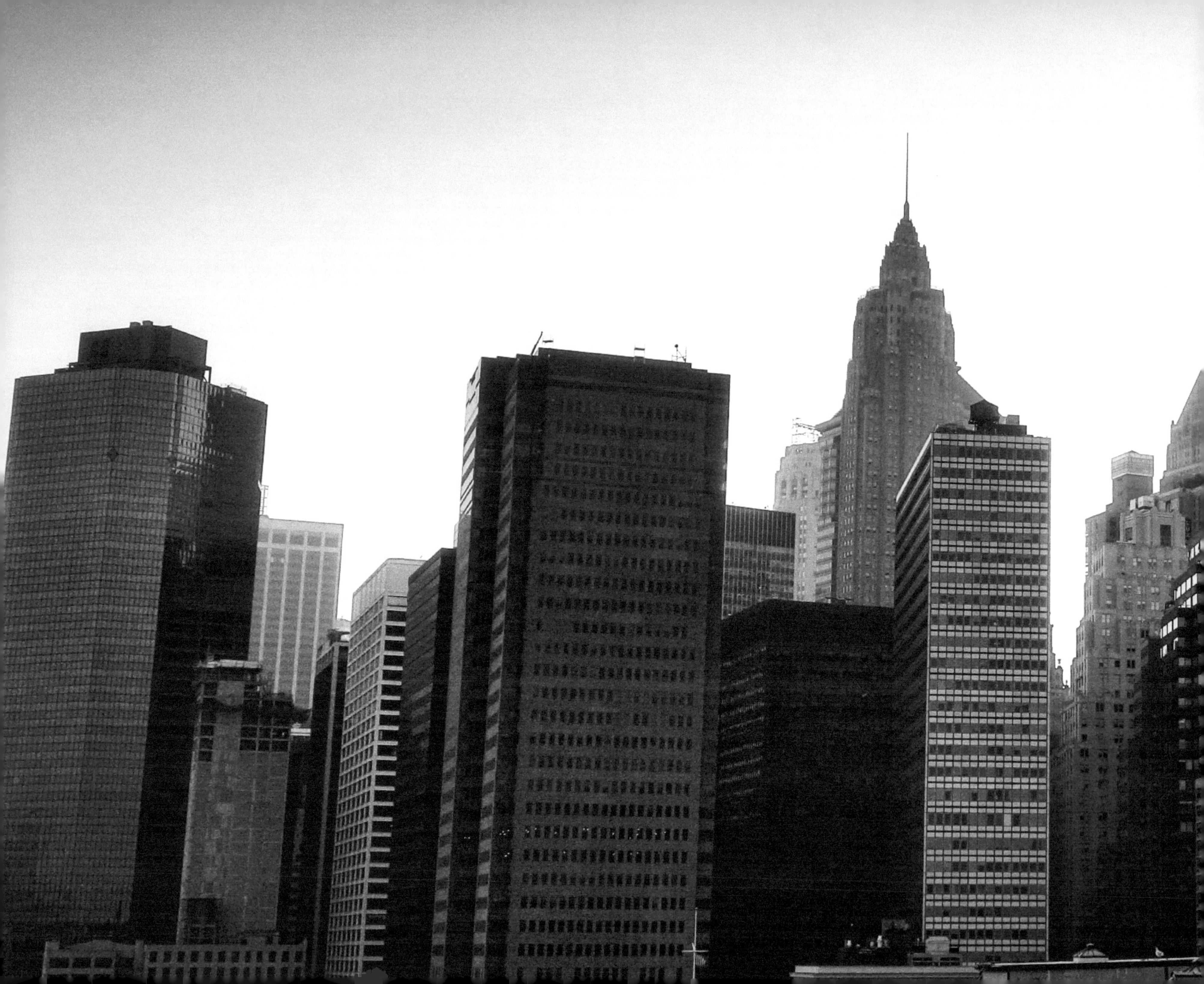

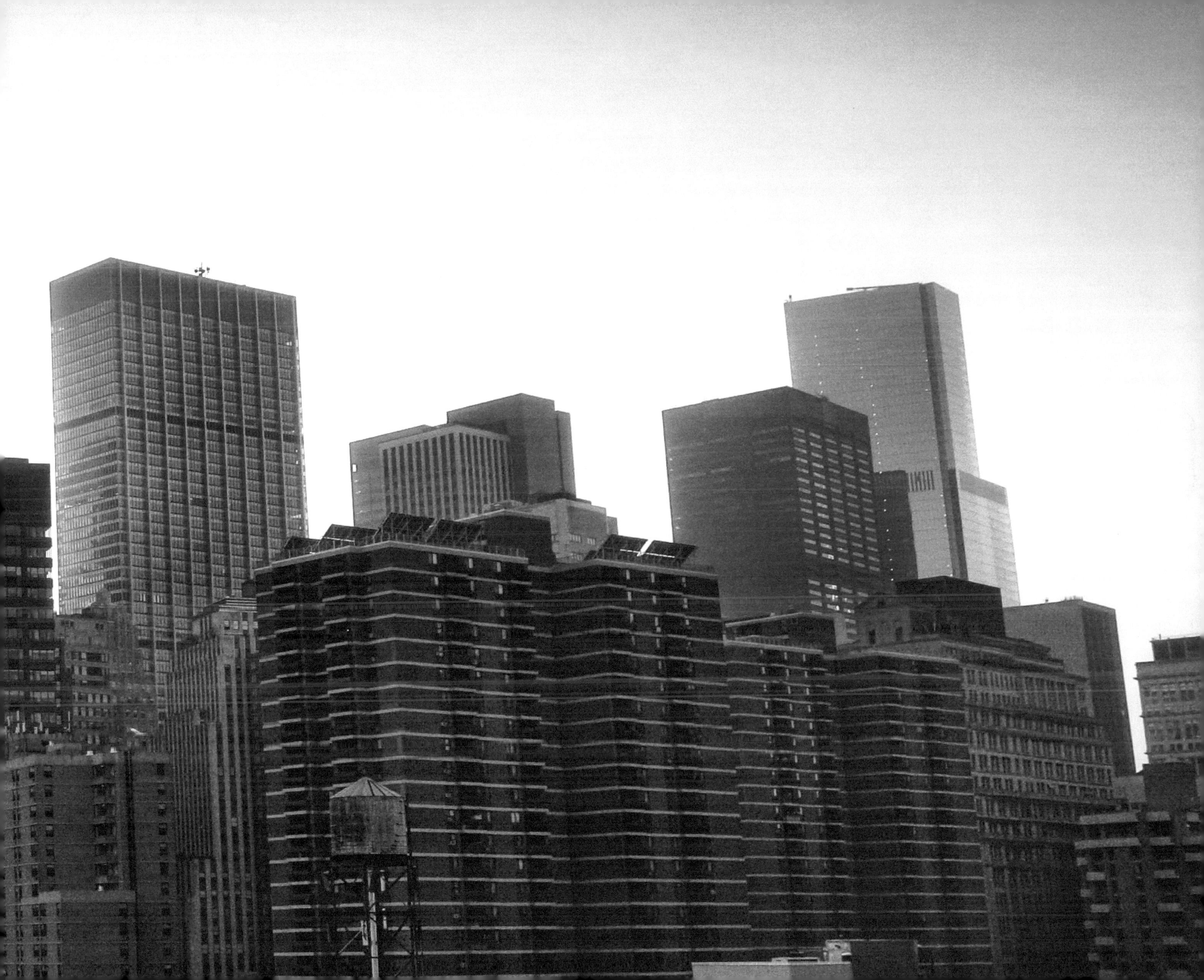

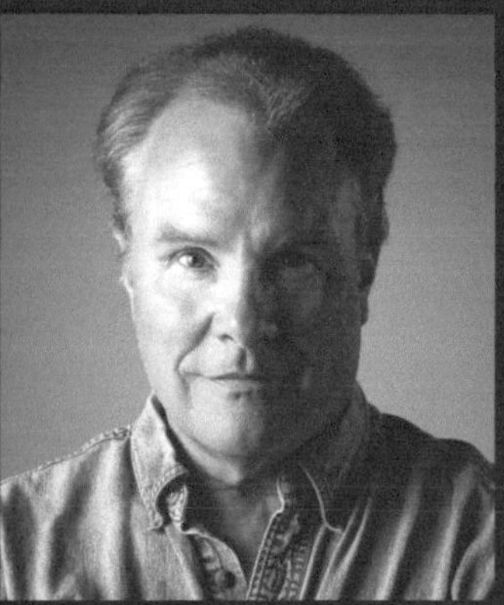

Christopher Briscoe lives in
La Jolla, California. He can
be reached through
www.chrisbriscoe.com or
www. shiftinggearspub.com

9 780989 940429